MAGNIFICENT

AUSTRALIA

MAGNIFICENT
AUSTRALIA

ROBERT COUPE

NEW
HOLLAND

First published in 1997 by
New Holland Publishers Pty Ltd
London · Cape Town · Sydney · Singapore

Produced and published in Australia by
New Holland Publishers Pty Ltd
3/2 Aquatic Drive, Frenchs Forest
NSW 2086 Australia

24 Nutford Place
London W1H 6DQ
United Kingdom

80 McKenzie Street
Cape Town 8001
South Africa

ISBN 1 86436 221 9

Senior Designer **Trinity Fry**
Editors **Jane Maliepaard,**
Anouska Good, Joanne Holliman
DTP Cartographer **John Loubser**
Publishing Manager **Mariëlle Renssen**
Commissioning Manager **Averill Chase**
Picture Researchers **Bronwyn Rennex,**
Peter Barker

Reproduction by Unifoto (Pty) Ltd
Printing and binding by Tien Wah Press (Pte) Ltd

Half-title page Sydney's Harbour Bridge and famous Opera
House are both monumental feats of engineering.
Title page The Walls of China in Mungo National Park have
been eroded into strange shapes by wind and water erosion.
This page The spectacular Elliot Falls are in the Jardine River
National Park on the Cape York Peninsula in Queensland.
Contents page A lone surfer basks in the late-afternoon sun on
Palm Beach on the edge of the glittering Pacific Ocean.

CONTENTS

THE
AUSTRALIAN
CONTINENT

*A*ustralia consists of two principal landmasses: the vast expanse of the mainland, which covers an area of 7 613 969 square kilometres, and the island of Tasmania, with an area of 68 331 square kilometres. It is situated in the southern hemisphere between latitudes 10°41'S and 43°39'S and longitudes 113°09'E and 153°39'E.

Despite its status as the sixth largest country on earth, only about 18 million people live in Australia. People from many parts of the world have made their homes here, especially since the end of World War II when the government initiated a vigorous migration program to attract new settlers, mainly from Britain and Europe, but also from parts of the Middle East. Since the 1970s, large numbers of people from South-East Asia have also migrated, so that together with the indigenous Aboriginal population, Australian society now represents a uniquely varied racial and cultural mix.

For political and administrative purposes, Australia is divided into six states and two territories. The states are all former British colonies which federated on 1 January 1901 to form the Commonwealth of Australia. In 1909 a small area of south-eastern New South Wales, the country's most populous state, became the Australian Capital Territory, and was earmarked as the future seat of the Australian Government. Two years later northern South Australia became the Northern Territory. A few external territories, such as Lord Howe Island, are also under Australian control.

Australia is a parliamentary democracy, whose system of government has developed mainly from the British Westminster system. Australians elect their national government every three years. Voting is compulsory for all Australian citizens who are 18 years of age and over. As Australia is a constitutional monarchy, the reigning British monarch is still the symbolic Head of State. The head of the government, however, is the Prime Minister, who is the leader of the political party that commands a majority in the national parliament. Each state and territory also has it own government, which has responsibility for such local issues as public transport, school education and hospitals.

250 kilometres
200 miles

Torres Strait

SOUTH PACIFIC OCEAN

Badu Island *Moa Island*
Prince of Wales Island
Jardine River N.P.

Melville Island
Cobourg Peninsula
Wessel Islands
Bathurst Island
Cape Arnhem
Cape Grenville

Darwin
Weipa
Great

Cape Londonderry
Kakadu N.P.
Arnhem Land
Groote Eylandt
Gulf of Carpentaria

Pearce Point
Great Barrier Reef

Kununurra
Victoria River Downs
Cape York Peninsula
Lakefield N.P.
Cooktown

Kimberley Region
Mornington Island
Cape Tribulation N.P.
Daintree N.P.
Green Island
Kuranda
Cairns
Gordonvale

Coral Sea

Purnululu (Bungle Bungle) N.P.
Atherton Tableland
Mareeba

Dunk Island
Hinchinbrook Island
Great Palm Island
Magnetic Island

Tanami Desert
NORTHERN
Barkly Tableland
Gulf Savannah
Ingham
Townsville

Dividing
Charters Towers
Bowen

TERRITORY
Whitsunday Islands

Devils Marbles
Tennant Creek
Mount Isa
Barkly Tableland
Mackay

Range
Northumberland Islands
Long Island

Ormiston Gorge
Alice Springs
Longreach
Rockhampton
Heron Island
Gladstone

MacDonnell Ranges
Channel Country
Kings Canyon
Finke Gorge N.P.

Carnarvon Gorge N.P.
Great Sandy N.P.

Uluru–Katatjuta N.P.
Simpson Desert
QUEENSLAND
Bundaberg

Fraser Island
Maryborough

Birdsville
Sturts Stony Desert

Great Victoria Desert
Simpson Desert
Moreton Island

SOUTH
Redcliffe
Brisbane

AUSTRALIA
Coober Pedy
Strzelecki Desert
Toowoomba
North Stradbroke Island
Ipswich Southport
Darling Downs
Coolangatta Surfers Paradise

Lake Torrens N.P.
Lismore
Byron Bay

Nullarbor Plain
Yetman
Grafton

Woomera
Bourke
Warrumbungles
Coffs Harbour

Flinders Ranges
Tamworth
Range

Ceduna
Wilcannia
Warrumbungle N.P.
Port Macquarie

Red Rocks Point
Broken Hill
NEW SOUTH
Barrington Tops N.P.

Port Augusta
WALES
Murrumbidgee
Newcastle

Great Australian Bight
Willandra N.P.
Darling
The Blue Mountains
Dividing

Port Lincoln
Mungo N.P.
Cowra
Sydney

Cape Carnot
Mildura
Wollongong
Berry

Adelaide
Barossa Valley
Murray Bridge
A.C.T.
Canberra

Flinders Chase N.P.
Swan Hill
Kerang
Cooma
Kosciuszko N.P.

Kangaroo Island
Murray
VICTORIA
Great

Horsham
Grampians N.P.
Ballarat
Cape Howe

Mount Gambier
Melbourne
Ninety Mile Beach

Portland
Geelong
Port Campbell
Port Campbell N.P.
Great Ocean Road
Tasman Sea

Bass Strait
Flinders Island
King Island
Cape Barren Island

OCEAN

Cradle Mtn–Lake St Clair N.P.
Launceston

Queenstown
Maria Island

TASMANIA
Hobart

South West Cape
South East Cape

9

A
DISTINCTIVE
LAND

A DISTINCTIVE LAND

*A*ustralia is variously described as the world's smallest continent or its largest island, but whichever way you look at it, the Australian landmass is enormous. It covers more than 7.6 million square kilometres with a total coastline of just under 37 000 kilometres. In some places rocky and rugged, in others consisting of long stretches of unbroken sandy beaches, and liberally dotted with sheltered bays, harbours and inlets, this great expanse of coastline is either washed or pounded by the waters of three mighty oceans: the Pacific in the east, the Indian in the west, and the Southern in the south.

Australia also has the distinction of being the world's driest continent. The greatest part of its area consists of desert or semi-desert regions that long defied the efforts of early European settlers to explore and traverse them and which, despite several grandiose schemes to make them fertile, remain resolutely inhospitable to large-scale settlement. Only the Aborigines, Australia's indigenous inhabitants who occupied the continent for at least 40 000 years before the arrival of Europeans, managed to exploit the resources of the country's arid centre.

Australia, by and large, is a nation of urban dwellers. The vast majority of Australians inhabit the cities and large towns along the eastern, southern and south-western coastal fringes. For many of them, the sea is their playground and the beaches their element. The dry centre is like a foreign country, somewhere to visit once or twice in a lifetime, but essentially remote from daily concerns and lifestyles.

The centre – which is usually referred to as the outback – does, however, have both powerful emotional and symbolic significance. Ask almost any Australian to identify a typical Australian landscape and they will most likely choose the desert. Ask them to name the country's most renowned natural feature and nine out of ten will nominate Uluru (formerly known as Ayers Rock), the huge, evocative rocky monolith that rises majestically from the desert sands. Perhaps the phrases that most strongly characterise Australia in the popular imagination are those coined by the poet Dorothea Mackellar, who described it as 'a sunburnt country' and a 'wide brown land'.

Previous pages Uluru in the Northern Territory evokes the quintessential image of Australia.
Previous pages (inset) Victoria's dramatic coastline has been carved by the Southern Ocean.
Opposite This golf course on Ben Buckler Headland overlooks Sydney's famous Bondi Beach.

CLIMATE AND THE LANDSCAPE

From Australia's most northerly point, at the tip of Cape York in Queensland, to its most southerly point, South East Cape in Tasmania, is a distance of more than 4500 kilometres. From Steep Point in Western Australia, the most westerly location, to Cape Byron in northern New South Wales, the country's easternmost point, is a similar distance. Within these limits is an amazing variety of landscapes, a huge diversity of vegetation and wildlife and a strongly contrasting range of climatic zones.

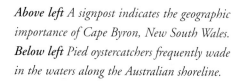

In Australia's tropical north the seasonal differences are between the 'wet' and the 'dry', but the weather is almost uniformly warm to hot the whole year round. The wet season brings tropical cyclones to coastal regions and monsoonal rains right across the north. In the north of Queensland are the lush, breathtakingly beautiful tropical and subtropical rainforests, which are home to an immense variety of animal and plant life. Further west in the Northern Territory are the wetlands of Kakadu National Park,

characterised by its famous escarpment and the various species of long-legged wading birds and other waterbirds as well as the ferociously predatory saltwater crocodile. Still further west, spanning the north-west tip of Western Australia and spilling over into the Northern Territory, are the magnificently rugged landscapes of the Kimberley with rocky gorges carved out by roaring streams in the wet season.

In the middle latitudes of the continent conditions are more temperate with most of the eastern and western seaboards enjoying what is often described as a 'Mediterranean' climate. The weather is characterised by warm summers and relatively mild winters. Only the high mountain areas in the alpine regions of southern New South Wales and northern Victoria, where Australia's ski resorts can be found, experience extreme winter conditions. These mountains form part of the Great Dividing Range, a series of mountains that runs continuously for the entire length of the eastern continent

Above left A signpost indicates the geographic importance of Cape Byron, New South Wales.
Below left Pied oystercatchers frequently wade in the waters along the Australian shoreline.

from North Queensland to south-western Victoria, and which also marks the western extremity of the coastal strip.

Situated just over 200 kilometres off the south-east corner of the mainland, and separated from it by the turbulent waters of the Bass Strait, is the island state of Tasmania. Its climate is influenced by the roaring forties, strong winds that blow eastwards across the southern Indian Ocean and Southern Ocean. These bring cool, moist air and cold winter temperatures to the island, especially to its spectacularly craggy alpine region in the rugged central plateau.

Above The highest mountain peaks lie within New South Wales' Kosciuszko National Park.
Below The twin peaks of Tasmania's Cradle Mountain overlook picturesque Dove Lake.

THE EVOLUTION FROM SUPERCONTINENT TO CONTINENT

Australia is not only the world's driest continent, it is also the flattest of all the landmasses. Even its highest, most recently formed mountains are small in comparison to the towering alps of Europe and Asia. Yet Australia was not always so flat and dry. Many of the rocky landforms in the centre of the continent that now fascinate us with their fantastic shapes and time-worn contours are remnants of once tall and extensive ranges, and as recently as 20 000–40 000 years ago much of the dry centre was a moist environment covered with lush vegetation.

Over the aeons, Australia has undergone changes that have moulded it into its present form. Continental drift, volcanic eruptions, earthquakes, glaciation, rising and falling sea levels and, more recently, the effects of human habitation have all played their part in shaping the continent.

Europeans in the first half of the 19th century were convinced that the centre of Australia was covered by a vast inland sea. Sadly, the explorers who went in search of it were a mere 150 million years too late. At that time the arid centre, now covered by sand or stone and vegetated mainly by spinifex and other spiky grasses, was a huge freshwater lake that scientists dubbed Lake Walloon. At the time the lake was thought to have existed, the continent was not yet a separate, identifiable landmass.

Australia once formed part of one of the world's two great supercontinents – Laurasia in the north and Gondwana in the south. About 150 million years ago the first rifts began to occur in Gondwana when South America and India started to drift away, 'floating' on tectonic plates at infinitesimal speed towards their present locations. Over the next 80 million years or so Africa and New Zealand also went their separate ways, leaving Australia and New Guinea still linked to the Antarctic landmass. It is conjectured that the final break-up occurred around 50 million years ago when Australia broke loose and began its inexorable journey northwards towards its current site. It would be another 25 million years before the continent assumed its present shape.

Above The Devils Marbles in the Northern Territory were once part of a single granite mass.
Right Queensland's Undara Lava Tubes were formed nearly 200 000 years ago by lava flow.

THE FIRST MIGRANTS

Most of the changes the Australian landmass underwent over the millenniums went unobserved by humans, although many land and marine animals, including numerous species of dinosaur, lived on the continent up to 220 million years ago. The forerunners of at least three of Australia's most characteristic animals – the wombat, the kangaroo and the emu – roamed parts of the continent as long as 2 million years ago.

Archaeological evidence suggests that it was not until around 40 000 to 60 000 years ago – more than 36 million years after the evolution of the first humans – that the early ancestors of Australia's Aborigines first came to these shores. Many Aborigines would dispute this because according to

their traditional beliefs, told in the stories of the Dreaming, Aborigines have lived on this land ever since it was first created. It is, however, generally thought that these 'first Australians' migrated from the South-East Asian region. They travelled by land and sea to the north of Australia and then spread south, east and west, settling in large family groups, or clans, and forming regional tribal boundaries. By about 20 000 years ago, all of the Australian continent and the island of Tasmania were populated by humans.

When the early Aborigines first arrived, Australia's climate and environment were

very different from what they are today, and its landmass was considerably more extensive. The continent was still joined to New Guinea in the north and Tasmania in the south. Large lakes covered much of the inland area, and the arid zones were much less widespread. Indeed, it was not until about 15 000 years ago that rising sea levels began to separate mainland Australia from Tasmania and New Guinea.

Aborigines adapted to the numerous climatic and environmental changes and a wealth of cultural and artistic traditions evolved. More than 200 Aboriginal languages developed, some of which,

despite considerable disruption to culture and traditions caused by European settlement and expansion, are still spoken today.

The Aborigines learned to exploit the resources of the land, rivers and sea, and to survive the harsh conditions that later proved inhospitable to Europeans. They also set in motion a process which continued and accelerated after the arrival of European settlers – that of manipulating the natural resources to suit human needs. With the use of fire, for example, Aborigines cleared areas of forest to facilitate hunting or to make some of the plants that they consumed more productive. When Europeans arrived on the continent a little over 200 years ago, there were, it is estimated, between 300 000 and 750 000 Aboriginal inhabitants in Australia.

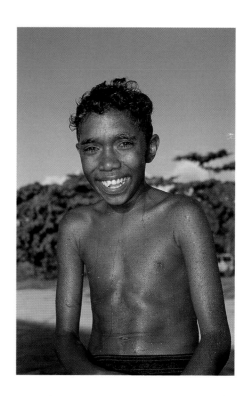

Above Aspects of Aboriginal life are unveiled at Cairns' Tjapukai Aboriginal Cultural Park.
Opposite The Aborigines' daily diet of plants was often supplemented by witchetty grubs.
Right Aborigines descend from many groups and kins, including Torres Strait Islanders.
Below Numerous Aboriginal rock art sites are evident in Carnarvon Gorge National Park.

Left *Biblioteca Apostolica Vaticana, Ms. Vat. Cat. 3811, fols.1–2: a Florentine version about* AD*1480 of a world map by the ancient Greek astronomer Ptolemy about* AD*150.*
Below *The Maritime Museum in Fremantle exhibits remains from the* Batavia, *a Dutch trader wrecked off Western Australia in 1629.*

NEW HOLLAND

By the early 17th century Holland had established itself as a formidable maritime power and controlled the Dutch East Indies, the islands that now make up Indonesia. In 1606, Willem Jansz sailed from Java in the *Duyfken* and landed on the Gulf of Carpentaria. It was the first authenticated European landing on Australian soil and the first contact with the land's inhabitants. In his report to authorities Jansz professed that 'no good was to be done' in this place.

The most significant Dutch exploration of Australia was undertaken by Abel Janszoon Tasman. In 1642 and again in 1644, Anthony Van Diemen, the Governor-General of the Dutch East Indies, sent Tasman on exploratory voyages south from the capital of Indonesia, Batavia (now Jakarta). On his first voyage Tasman sailed due south, then east, and was forced ashore

THE GREAT SOUTH LAND

Australia is often referred to as 'Down Under', a description Australians have, by and large, happily accepted. The concept, a modern-day re-emergence of the centuries-old European idea that a great southern continent existed, is thought to have originated from the ancient Greek astronomer Ptolemy who, in AD150, drew a world map showing a mass of land in the south to balance the known world in the north. He named this imaginary land *Terra Australis Incognita* – 'unknown southern land'.

During the 16th century, the Spanish and the Portuguese vied with each other to be the first to discover the great south land that everyone believed existed but which many feared was inhabited by monsters. In 1605, in a memorable voyage that might have changed the course of Australian history, the Spaniard Pedro Fernandez de Quiros led an expedition from Lima in Peru and landed on one of the islands that are now known as Vanuatu. He believed he had discovered the elusive south land. Faced with a mutinous crew, de Quiros returned home and left the

remaining ships under the command of Luis Vaez de Torres to continue the voyage westwards. Torres turned north before reaching the east coast of Australia, sailed through the strait between Cape York and New Guinea and ended up in the Philippines at the site of present-day Manila. He came very close to landing on the east coast of Australia.

A LAND 'DESTITUTE OF WATER'

If Willem Jansz was unimpressed with the continent he found, the first Englishman to set foot on Australian land was similarly unenthusiastic. In 1688 the adventurer and pirate William Dampier landed on the north-west coast, about 200 kilometres north of where the town of Broome now stands, in search of fresh water. On his return to England, he wrote a book in which he described what he saw:

'New Holland is a very large Tract of Land ...The Land is of a dry Sandy soil, destitute of Water, except you make Wells... There was pretty long Grass growing under the Trees; but it was very thin. We saw no Trees that bore Fruit or Berries. We saw no sort of Animal, nor any track of Beast, but once; and that seemed to be the tread of a Beast as big as a great Mastiff-Dog. Here are a few small Land-birds, but none bigger than a Blackbird: and but a few Sea-fowls.'

Dampier's impressions of the land still reflect the initial reactions to the Australian landscape by many Europeans today. Visitors from the northern hemisphere are often disconcerted by what they perceive as the harshness of the country, by the scrubbiness of much of its bush, and by the greyish-green foliage and rough-hewn bark of the predominant tree species, the eucalyptus. Early European painters sought to compensate the antipodean landscapes by depicting them in terms of the British notion of picturesque. The greens became darker, the foliage thicker, the light muted, and skies were made darker and smaller. The vast, rugged beauty of much of Australia is, for many, still an acquired taste.

by bad weather. He landed at a place subsequently called Storm Bay near the southern tip of Tasmania. The navigator named the island Van Diemen's Land after his patron. On his second voyage Tasman sailed due east until stormy weather again played a hand and forced him south. Failing to pass through Torres Strait (named after Luis Vaez de Torres), he sighted and charted the western side of Cape York, around the Gulf of Carpentaria, the north and north-west coast of the continent and a large portion of the west coast of Australia. He named this tract of land New Holland.

For another 200 years, European maps labelled the new continent, or as much of it as was known, under the name Tasman had pronounced. A Dutch map of 1660 shows an accurate depiction of most of the north coast, the entire west coast and about half of the southern coast. Cape York is shown to merge with the island of New Guinea and the east coast remains a mysterious blank.

Above *The Tasman Fountain in Hobart was named in honour of the famous Dutch explorer.*
Top right *Majestic river red gums are the most commonly known of Australia's eucalypts.*
Right *William Dampier landed just north of Gantheaume Bay near the town of Broome.*

A MIGHTY ENDEAVOUR

Despite its adverse tone, Dampier's report stimulated official British interest in New Holland. In 1699 the Admiralty sent him back to explore further. Dampier reached the west coast of Australia at an inlet that he named Shark Bay, which is now famous for its tame dolphins at Monkey Mia and for the stromatolites (stone-like living organisms that date back 3500 million years) at Hamelin Pool. Dampier then sailed north as far as the site of his former landing but was no more impressed than before. His plans to investigate the Australian coastline further were thwarted by the deteriorating seaworthiness of his ship, the *Roebuck*.

British interest was kindled, but the best part of a century was to pass before another expedition was organised. This time it was entrusted to Captain James Cook, sent ostensibly on a scientific mission to observe the transit of Venus on the Pacific island of Tahiti. In addition to this task Cook received separate orders from the British Admiralty to continue sailing west to unravel the remaining mysteries surrounding New Holland, the great south land. On 19 April 1770, just short of 20 months after leaving England, Zachary Hicks, Captain Cook's first lieutenant on the HM Barque *Endeavour*, sighted the point that now bears his name, Point Hicks, on the south-eastern coast of Australia.

For four months, the *Endeavour* sailed north along Australia's east coast. During this time, Cook charted the coastline and named places after British notables, natural features or, sometimes, after incidents that occurred in that place. Botany Bay, just south of the present-day Sydney, was where plant specimens were collected; Port Jackson, the site of Sydney's harbour, was named after a British naval official; Moreton Bay, near Brisbane, was named after an organiser of the expedition; the treacherous Whitsunday Passage between the mainland and islands of the now famed Great Barrier Reef was negotiated on Whit Sunday; and Cape Tribulation marks the spot near where the

Endeavour struck a coral reef on 11 June. The crippled ship beached on the shores of the Endeavour River to be repaired before Cook could continue his travels north to Cape York, named in honour of the Duke of York. On 22 August 1770, Captain Cook raised the British flag on Possession Island at the tip of Cape York, thereby claiming the entire east coast of Australia as a British territory. He named it New South Wales.

Above In 1770, Captain Cook proclaimed the whole east coast of Australia as British.
Left Cooktown in north Queensland honours James Cook with a statue looking out to sea.
Below, from left A replica of the Endeavour *was built for Australia's bicentenary in 1988; Cook recommended Botany Bay as a site for settlement; a monument stands on Possession Island where the proclamation was made.*

SETTLEMENT AND EXPANSION

Eighteen years after Cook's exploration and proclamation of the east coast of Australia, a fleet of ships sailed into Botany Bay carrying nearly 1500 people to set up a British penal colony. Just over half of the passengers on board were convicted British felons, both male and female. The remainder were British soldiers and officials.

On Cook's recommendation, Botany Bay had been chosen as the site of the colony but the expedition's leader and the colony's first governor, Captain Arthur Phillip, found the bay unsuitable. He sailed further north and entered Port Jackson, which he described as 'the finest harbour in the world, in which a thousand ships of the line may ride in the most perfect security' – a description with which modern Sydneysiders still proudly concur. As the site of his settlement, Phillip chose a sheltered bay within Port Jackson, which he named Sydney Cove after Lord Sydney. On 26 January 1788 the 11 ships of the First Fleet, as they henceforth became known, relocated their motley human cargo to the site which is now the bustling ferry terminus called Circular Quay.

Above right Sydney Cove, the site of the first European settlement in Australia, is marked by the Opera House and Harbour Bridge.
Right A statue of Governor Phillip is the focus of a fountain in Sydney's Botanic Gardens.
Below The South Head peninsula forms the southern arm of the entrance to Port Jackson.

By the end of the 18th century Australia had revealed to Europeans most of the secrets about its shape and extent. Its content, however, still remained a mystery, and for more than a quarter of a century after the first European settlement, the door to the vast interior remained locked. That door was the Great Dividing Range, about 50 kilometres inland from the coast, and the key to it was the Blue Mountains, lying directly west of the settlement of Port Jackson.

The Blue Mountains, so named because of the blue haze – the result of distilled eucalyptus oil – that surrounds them when viewed from a distance, is an area of spectacular and still largely unspoilt natural beauty. Its heights are modest but its plateaus are cut by deep valleys with sheer sandstone precipices and plunging waterfalls. To the early settlers these mountains presented an impenetrable barrier and a frustrating limitation to settlement and expansion. Expedition after expedition ventured into these valleys, only to be stopped in their tracks by sheer cliffs that prevented the plateaus from being scaled.

In 1813 the explorers Blaxland, Lawson and Wentworth found a way across by following the ridges, rather than the valleys. A settlement sprang up at Bathurst, on the western slopes of the mountains. This became the starting point for a number of expeditions that eventually unravelled the mysteries of the inland rivers and opened up routes to the north and south of the continent. The establishment of widespread farming and pastoral activities followed.

New settlements around the coast became the capital cities of first the separate British colonies, and then of the Australian states. These cities also provided springboards for excursions into the interior and by the mid-1860s the north of the continent had been traversed, south to north crossings of the continent had been accomplished, and the nature of Australia's arid centre was

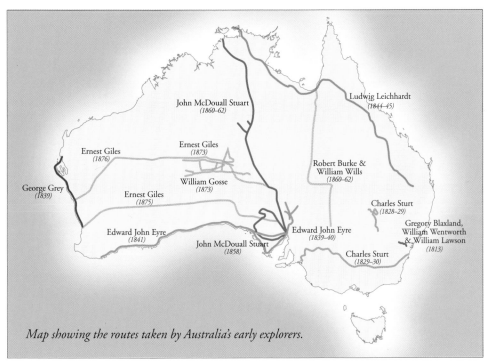

Map showing the routes taken by Australia's early explorers.

well understood. It was not, however, until 1873 that William Gosse, on a surveying expedition in central Australia, happened upon Australia's most familiar landmark which he named after Sir Henry Ayers, a former premier of the state of South Australia and which is now known by its original Aboriginal name, Uluru.

Above *Known to Aborigines since prehistoric times, Uluru was 'discovered' in 1873 by William Gosse who named it Ayers Rock.*
Left *Many explorers traversed the Australian continent, opening the vast land to settlement.*
Opposite *The steep sandstone escarpments that are a feature of the Blue Mountains were a formidable barrier to early explorers.*

FLORA AND FAUNA

Millions of years of isolation from the rest of the earth's landmasses meant that Australia evolved a unique flora and fauna. Two botanists, Sir Joseph Banks and Daniel Solander, were part of Cook's expedition along the east coast. During their periods ashore they collected more than 10 000 specimens of Australian plants. Among them were examples of a most distinctive plant species, to which Banks gave his name. With their large bottlebrush flowers and rough-edged grey-green leaves, banksias are one of the most widespread and instantly recognisable plants in Australia. Along with other native species such as grevilleas and wattles, which in early spring bear brilliant yellow blooms, and the ubiquitous eucalyptus, or gum tree as it is more commonly known, banksias give much of the Australian landscape its characteristic look.

William Dampier, too, in his visits almost a century earlier, had collected a number of plant specimens. One of these was a ground-hugging wildflower with a

brilliant scarlet bloom which he described as 'looking very beautiful'. This flower, the Sturt's desert pea, named after the inland explorer Charles Sturt, is one of the many wildflowers that thrive even in the arid centre. After heavy rains, these plants can turn a desert area into a riot of brilliant colours, relieving the monotony of the spiky spinifex grasses and stunted grey saltbushes.

Below Koalas live in the tops of trees and exist almost exclusively on a diet of gum leaves.

Above Kangaroos rear their young in a pouch, and can be seen in most areas of Australia.

HOW THE EMU LOST ITS WINGS AND THE KOOKABURRA GAINED ITS LAUGH

Aboriginal myths, also known collectively as the Dreaming, often explain how the natural world came to be as it is. This particular story is told by several tribes that live along the Murray River.

In times long past, emus soared in the sky high above the earth. One day an emu flew close to the ground and, seeing that others were living there, decided to land and investigate. She met a group of brolgas — long-legged water birds that are famous for their elegant dance-like movements — and asked their permission to stay and live on earth. The brolgas, as mischievous as they are graceful, tucked their huge wings in against their bodies and told the emu that her wings were far too large for a ground-dweller; she would have to cut them off if she were to move around on earth without bumping into everything. Reluctantly the emu shed her generous wings, only to see the brolgas suddenly spread their magnificent wings and fly off majestically, leaving the poor emu flightless and stranded.

A kookaburra, who was sitting on a nearby tree, was witness to the scene. He was so amused by it that he burst into peals of uproarious mirth. When he regained control of himself, he flew off to tell his companions who, on hearing his tale, also exploded into spontaneous laughter. Since then, kookaburras have laughed loud and long every time they think about the trick played by the cunning brolgas on the trusting, but unfortunate, emu.

Above The common brush-tailed possum loves the leaves, fruit and flowers of suburban plants. *Below* There are over 20 species of goanna in Australia and some grow up to 2 metres long.

Above There are over 100 species of banksia in Australia, all featuring rough-edged leaves. At certain times of the year, these hardy little plants exhibit brilliantly coloured blooms.

Above The raucous-laughing kookaburra inhabits Australia's east and south-east parts. *Below* The short-beaked echidna forages for insects at night, and is rarely seen in the wild.

Many species of mammals, reptiles and birds that exist in Australia are unlike animals anywhere else in the world. Unfortunately, the chances of a visitor encountering them in the wild are slim as most are nocturnal and many, including the cuddly-looking but sharp-clawed koala, inhabit the upper reaches of gum trees. However, groups of bounding kangaroos or their close relatives, the wallabies, may be encountered during a drive along a country road, especially at dusk. It was almost certainly a kangaroo's tracks that Dampier wrote about in his diary in 1688. These mammals belong to a specialised group called marsupials, which are unique to

Australia and parts of South America. The group includes koalas, possums, wombats, bandicoots and the Tasmanian Devil.

When marsupials are born they are still in an embryonic state and live in a pouch on their mother's abdomen until they reach full development. Young kangaroos, fondly referred to as joeys, live in their mother's pouch for about 18 months.

Australia's most unusual mammals are the duck-billed platypus, which lives in muddy burrows along river banks, and the spiky echidna, which lives exclusively on a diet of ants. The platypus and echidna are two of only three monotremes – egg-laying mammals – that exist anywhere in the world. The other is another type of echidna that lives in New Guinea.

There are reputed to be 750 species of native birds in Australia, many of them unique to the country. They range from the large, dull-coloured, flightless but fleet-footed emu to tiny finches and robins. Many, such as numerous species of parrot, are spectacularly coloured. The Australian bush

often rings with the sounds of bird calls, some of them harsh and raucous, others sweetly melodious. The most distinctive sounds are undoubtedly the superb carolling of the magpie and the maniacal-sounding call of the laughing kookaburra.

Australia's reptiles are both weird and wonderful, from the famed and justly feared saltwater crocodile that lives in northern rivers to more than 500 species of lizard of all shapes, sizes and colours. Lizards live everywhere in Australia, from verdant rain-forests to the driest of desert areas. While many of them are fearsome in appearance, they are generally harmless and add to the richness of Australia's natural environment.

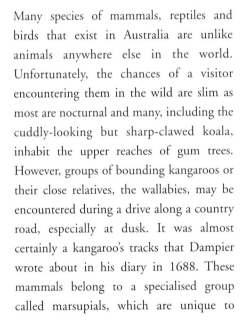

AUSTRALIA'S

CAPITAL

CITIES

AUSTRALIA'S CAPITAL CITIES

*P*olitically and administratively Australia is divided into six states and two territories. Five of the state capitals – Brisbane, Sydney, Melbourne, Adelaide, Perth – and Darwin, the administrative centre of the Northern Territory, are dotted around the coastal fringe of the mainland, while Hobart lies in the south-east of the island state of Tasmania. Canberra, the national capital and the only inland capital, occupies a tiny region called the Australian Capital Territory, which lies within the state of New South Wales. Almost two-thirds of Australia's population of nearly 18 million people live in the six state capitals.

Except for Canberra, which was built in the 1920s, and Darwin, whose growth has been largely undertaken in the postwar years, all of Australia's capitals began in the 19th century as British colonies and centres of regional government. Sydney, Australia's oldest and largest city, was founded as a convict settlement in 1788. In 1804 and 1825 respectively, Hobart and Brisbane began life under similarly inauspicious circumstances. The other capitals were founded as free settlements – Perth in 1829, Melbourne in 1835 and Adelaide in 1836. The six colonies united and became states within the newly formed Commonwealth of Australia in 1901.

Australia's capitals are vibrant modern cities that reflect both their colonial beginnings and the dramatic changes that have transformed Australian society in the years since World War II. Most of them show an often pleasing blend of architectural styles, combining recent high-rise offices and residential buildings with the sandstone Victorian and early 20th-century dwellings. The population of the different cities reveals the changes in the waves of immigrations – first from Britain, then from central and southern Europe and the Middle East, and more recently from Asia – that have transformed Australian cities from overwhelmingly Anglo-Celtic strongholds into cosmopolitan centres.

The different cuisine – from European to Asian – that the multitude of ethnic backgrounds have brought with them, the warm weather that has sanctioned outdoor eating venues, and the cultural successes that Australian artists have enjoyed, have all contributed to the genuinely international ambience of the continent's capital cities.

Previous pages From the Harbour Bridge, the views across Australia's oldest city are magical.
Previous pages (inset) Darwin's new six-level Parliament House is illuminated as dusk falls.
Opposite An elaborate flagpole sits astride Parliament House on Capital Hill in Canberra.

THE HARBOUR CITY

Few cities have a finer natural setting than Sydney, the capital of New South Wales, whose harbour has inspired generations of painters and photographers to capture its beauty and its changing moods. The harbour defines Sydney in much the same way that the canals define Venice. The harbour is also the focus of much of Sydney's commercial and recreational activity. On a summer's afternoon it is alive with colour and movement as large ocean liners, cruise ships, huge container ships and oil tankers sail majestically through the Heads that form the harbour's entrance and steam beneath the bridge on their way to their respective berths. Pleasure craft and racing yachts bob between the larger craft and share the ample waterways with a variety of commuter ferries linking the city's Circular Quay with harbourside and riverside suburbs. A ferry or hydrofoil trip north to Manly, a suburb occupying a narrow strip of land between the harbour and the ocean, offers the visitor an ideal opportunity to sample the harbour and enjoy its scenic splendour. Sydney's two most potent symbols are integrally associated with the harbour: the Sydney Harbour Bridge, the soaring steel arches of which have linked the harbour's north and south shores since 1932; and the Sydney Opera House, designed with gleaming white shells suggestive of billowing sails, and which stands at a prominent point on the water's edge. Both occupying prime positions at the entrance to Sydney Cove, these are perhaps Australia's most internationally famed structures. Stretching southwards from Circular Quay at Sydney Cove is the central business district. Since the 1960s high-rise buildings have transformed the city's skyline, turning many of the streets into wind tunnels but providing superb vistas of the harbour from their lofty heights, none better than the 360-degree panorama from the top of the Sydney Tower.

Above As darkness descends, the massive arch of Sydney Harbour Bridge is illuminated by floodlights, showing the full glory of its engineered span. *Opposite* Gleaming in the sunlight, the multiple sail-shaped roofs of the Sydney Opera House are composed of over a million white ceramic tiles. *Following pages* Sydney has grown in just over 200 years from a small penal settlement on the outskirts of the world into a thriving metropolis.

THE OPERA HOUSE AND HARBOUR BRIDGE

Approaching Sydney by water, one is confronted simultaneously by two of Australia's most famous icons: the Sydney Harbour Bridge, an engineering marvel, which was opened in 1932 during the Great Depression; and the Sydney Opera House, often called the greatest building of the 20th century.

Opened in 1973, the Sydney Opera House was fraught with strife and controversy over its 14-year construction period. In 1966, with the exterior of the building still largely incomplete, its Danish architect, Jørn Utzon, whose innovative design had been chosen in 1957 as the result of an international design competition, resigned from the project, leaving the interior to be completed by a team of local architects.

The Opera House, or performing arts complex, comprises a large timber-panelled concert hall, that seats 2700 people, and a smaller opera theatre, which is used for opera and ballet and can accommodate about 1500 people. There are two additional theatres used for drama, which are both situated beneath the concert hall: the black-walled Drama Theatre and the smaller, more intimate Playhouse.

The Sydney Harbour Bridge is a single-span arch bridge which took eight years to build. Its deck is 59 metres above the water and it is supported by an arch measuring 503 metres. The bridge was manufactured, section by section, on a site near its northern end and the arch was built simultaneously from both ends until the two halves finally met in the middle.

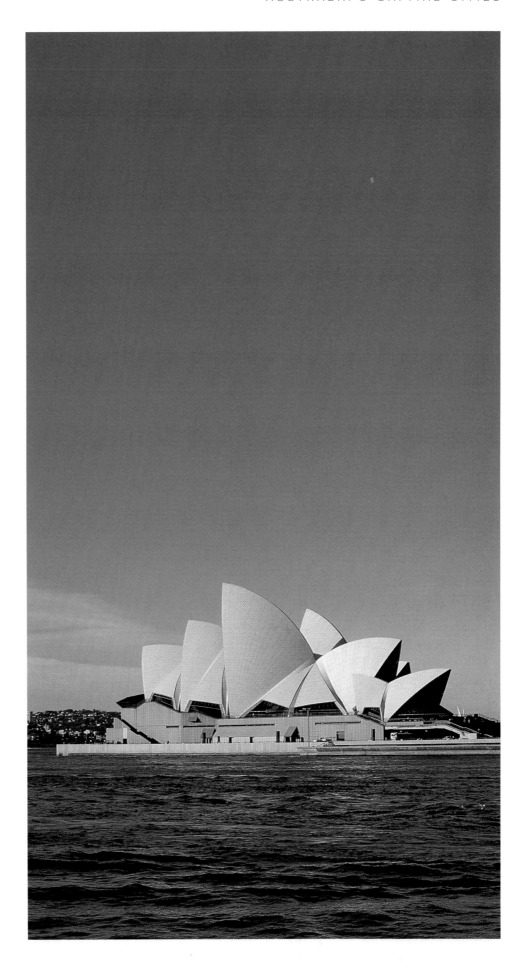

Above *The National Maritime Museum at Darling Harbour has thousands of exhibits.*

Above *Darling Harbour is linked to Sydney's city centre by a monorail that offers great views.*

Above *At the Sydney Aquarium, the exciting Open Ocean exhibit has underwater tunnels.*

Throughout Sydney's business district are numerous reminders of Sydney's convict era as well as an impressive collection of handsome mid- to late-Victorian buildings. Macquarie Street, which was once described as 'the most beautiful street in the British Empire', contains several examples of the work of the prolific convict-architect Francis Greenway. At the southern end of the street, opposite each other, are the graceful Georgian St James Church and the beautifully restored Hyde Park Barracks, now an historical museum. Within view of both of these buildings is the huge Gothic-Revival cathedral of St Mary's, the main church of the Catholic Archdiocese of Sydney.

On George Street there are three fine but contrasting Victorian buildings. Sydney's other Victorian cathedral, St Andrew's, has slender, graceful lines and seems diffidently to turn its back on the hustle of the traffic-laden street and to keep its towers and large west window away from the public gaze. Right next to it, and unashamedly presenting its façade to George Street, is the Sydney Town Hall, unkindly dubbed the 'wedding cake' by those who find its mass of carved stone decoration excessive, but which is a fine expression of 19th-century taste. The last building in the trio is the massive Queen Victoria Building. With its copper domes, cupolas, classical statues and carved sandstone exterior, it is almost impossible to believe that barely a quarter of a century ago this superb example of late-Victorian architecture was a candidate for demolition. Now beautifully restored as an elegant multi-gallery shopping centre, which houses fashionable boutiques, cafes and restaurants, it has become a major thoroughfare for city pedestrians and is one of the city's top tourist attractions.

Below *On perfect summer days, crowds of people are attracted to Bondi Beach, which is located only eight minutes by car from the city centre.*

Below *Balmoral Beach, an expanse of white sand and rocky outcrops on the harbour's northern shoreline, is ideal for families with young children.*

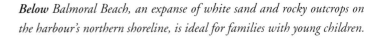

Above The sandstone façade of the Town Hall, likened to a wedding cake, is intricately detailed.

Above The Gothic-Revival St Mary's Roman Catholic Cathedral boasts an imposing nave.

Above An archway flanked by Chinese lions marks the entrance to Sydney's Chinatown.

Past the northern façade of the Queen Victoria Building and, for many, inexcusably obscuring that building's elegant line, is the elevated carriageway for Sydney's monorail. The monorail's sleek cars convey passengers between stops within the city to Sydney's most recently created public space, Darling Harbour. Whereas parts of Sydney evoke its past, Darling Harbour is all modernity. Opened in 1988, it was developed from a long-disused dockyard into a landscaped open space surrounded by futuristic white structures which house exhibition halls, conference centres and a plethora of shops and restaurants as well as the Sydney Aquarium, the National Maritime Museum and the Chinese Garden. Darling Harbour was a controversial development but its large open space and myriad activities have proved a magnet for the inhabitants of the city.

In contrast, The Rocks, situated on the western side of Sydney Cove directly opposite the Opera House, has succeeded in retaining its old-world charm. For much of the 19th century and into the 20th, The Rocks was a crowded slum, a breeding ground for disease and a place notorious for street crime. It has been restored to an ordered and charming urban village which re-creates, to a large extent, the ambience of early Sydney. Its terrace houses, storehouses, pubs and narrow lanes and alleyways can still be experienced by strolling along Nurses Walk and Suez Canal – a pun on the former name, Sewer's Canal. For many visitors the focus of a visit to The Rocks is the Argyle Centre, a rambling old storehouse that once housed contraband goods but which is now a vibrant art and craft centre selling everything from souvenirs to skilfully crafted woodwork, glassware and jewellery.

Below The stalls at the weekend market in The Rocks area at the northern end of George Street sell many unusual Australian art and craft items.

Below Named after Robert Campbell, the beautifully restored Campbell's Warehouse near Sydney Cove now houses popular waterfront restaurants.

MARVELLOUS MELBOURNE

While Sydney was founded as a convict settlement, Melbourne, capital of Victoria, came into being as a result of a piece of blatant chicanery. In 1835, John Batman arrived from Van Diemen's Land and purchased from local Aborigines, for a few paltry trinkets, an area of 243 000 hectares at the head of Port Phillip Bay in Victoria. He described the area as 'a deep river of several miles running with fresh water. This is the place for a village'. Governor Burke declared the purchase illegal, a decree promptly ignored by squatters and settlers who eagerly began to set up home beside the Yarra, the name the Aborigines had given the river. Batman's partner in the enterprise, John Pascoe Fawkner, soon afterwards built Melbourne's first building, a grog shop.

Comparisons between Sydney and Melbourne are inevitable and are kindled by the traditional rivalry between the two cities. One area of strong contrast is in the layout of the cities' central areas. Sydney was essentially unplanned, with much of its business district consisting of narrow streets that simply grew up haphazardly along bush tracks. In 1837, however, the city of Melbourne was surveyed and laid out according to a logical and regular grid system. Central Melbourne is a model of forward planning, its well-defined blocks and more generously proportioned streets providing an air of elegance that is sometimes lacking in its more congested northerly sister. No street vista in Sydney quite matches the view looking north-east along Bourke Street with trams running up and down the steep incline and

Opposite The Flinders Street Railway Station is a flamboyant reminder of the wealth that characterised the city during the Victorian era.
Above right The Yarra winds its way through the city, passing under the Princes Bridge not far from the white spire of the Victorian Arts Centre.
Below The spectacular floodlit Flinders Street Railway Station and Melbourne's towering skyscrapers glow in the early evening light.

the Bourke Street Mall in the middle distance. An avenue of trees frames the majestic façade of Victoria's Parliament House, which is backed by the soaring towers of St Patrick's Cathedral.

Much of Melbourne's modern elegance derives from its surviving Victorian buildings, the result of the gold rushes that brought enormous wealth to the city in the 1850s and 1860s as well as the growth that came from the establishment of pastoral properties in its environs. Melbourne's growth and prosperity continued right up to the 1880s and for most of the late 1800s its population exceeded Sydney's. The description 'marvellous Melbourne' became current at this time of rapid development. Proud reminders of the era include the huge Flinders Street Railway Station, with its lofty clock tower and grand domed entrance; the city's two Gothic-Revival cathedrals – the Anglican St Paul's, opened in 1891 and the Catholic St Patrick's, constructed over a 21-year period from 1858; the elegant Princess Theatre built in 1886; and the General Post Office building, which was completed in 1867 although its tower was not added until 1889.

High-rise development has greatly altered the skyline and ambience of Melbourne since the 1960s. One notable development that has enhanced the city, both architecturally and culturally, is the Arts

Above Sculptures adorn a hairdressing salon in fashionable St Kilda, South Melbourne.

Above Part of a display that appears above a flower shop in Brunswick Street in Fitzroy.

Above Faithfully restored century-old bathing boxes at Brighton Beach on Port Phillip Bay.

Centre complex, a handsome modern circular white building with a flamboyant steel tower and spacious riverside site. The Victorian Arts Centre is Melbourne's main focus of dramatic and musical life and houses the National Gallery of Victoria. Nearby is Southgate, Melbourne's 'left bank', a bustling venue with waterfront restaurants and cafes and a large range of shops. Southgate also joins up with Melbourne's new Casino and the Polly Woodside Maritime Museum.

Expansive parks and gardens occupy large areas of the central city area. Perhaps most impressive of all is the beautifully landscaped Royal Botanic Gardens. Adjoining the Botanic Gardens is the vast Kings Domain where Government House, the official residence of the governor of Victoria, stands, and the green expanse where the city's impressive Shrine of Remembrance overlooks busy St Kilda Road.

Melbourne has welcomed immigrants from all parts of the world and is now a vital cosmopolitan centre. Greeks form the largest immigrant group in Melbourne – indeed it is claimed that Melbourne has the largest Greek population of any city except Athens – but it is the Italians that have had the most conspicuous influence on Melbourne's restaurant scene. For almost three decades, no visit to the city could be considered complete without a visit to Carlton, an inner-city suburb, or a stroll along Lygon Street, which is lined with restaurants offering every kind of traditional Italian fare.

Below Crammed with reasonably priced ethnic eateries and busy pubs, Brunswick Street is typical of Fitzroy, an inner-city suburb of Melbourne. *Below right* The Yarra River, which flows through the bustling heart of the city centre, provides a perfect setting for summer rowing regattas.

Opposite Designed by Melbourne architect Roy Grounds, the Victorian Arts Centre, on the south bank of the Yarra River, comprises several buildings. The most spectacular is the main theatre complex, housing the Playhouse and the State Theatre, which is surmounted by a steel tower.

Above *Opened in 1988, the New Parliament House was built on top of Capital Hill, and is the central focus of the city of Canberra.*
Left *The Telstra Tower on Black Mountain is another prominent landmark in Canberra and provides spectacular views of the city.*
Right *The Captain Cook Memorial Water Jet in the middle of Lake Burley Griffin shoots water up to 140 metres into the air.*
Below *Looking down Anzac Avenue from the Australian War Memorial, both the new and the old Parliament House buildings are visible.*
Opposite *Panoramic views of Canberra and the surrounding Australian Capital Territory countryside can be seen from Black Mountain.*

A CITY ON A LAKE

In a sense Canberra, Australia's national capital, is a direct offspring of the famous Sydney–Melbourne rivalry. It may have seemed logical for either Sydney or Melbourne to become the national capital after the federation of Australia officially came into existence in 1901, but neither city's authorities would yield to the other. A site somewhere else had to be found and, ideally, that location had to be not too close to either Sydney or Melbourne. As a result, the Molonglo Valley in southern New South Wales was chosen as the site of the Australian Capital Territory, and an international competition was held for the design of the new federal city. Walter Burley Griffin, an American architect, was the winner and it was out of his vision, and largely conforming to the spirit of his design, that Canberra grew.

The dominant feature is an artificial lake, Lake Burley Griffin, named after the city's designer but not completed until 1961 when the Molonglo River was finally dammed. On either side of the lake are perhaps the city's most prominent landmarks. Ingeniously built into the side of Capital Hill, without seeming to dominate it, is Parliament House, which was opened in 1988. This is the seat of the federal government of Australia. Down the slope in front of it, on the same side of the lake, is an elegant white building that previously housed parliament from 1927. On the other side of the lake at the end of the long, broad, tree-lined Anzac Avenue is the domed Australian War Memorial, a vital museum which records and re-creates aspects of Australia's involvement in conflicts, including the two World Wars.

Along the shores of Lake Burley Griffin are the High Court of Australia and the Australian National Gallery, which opened in 1968 and which contains the nation's most extensive collection of modern and colonial Australian art as well as an impressive collection of international art. At regular intervals the National Gallery mounts major travelling art exhibitions that attract large numbers of visitors. Also on the lakeside is the National Library, the classic Greek lines of which contrast, but also blend, with the contemporary style of the Gallery and High Court.

The city's 'centre' is contained in a small area known as Civic, which has developed around two colonnaded blocks dating back to the 1920s. However, many services and government departments are located in numerous suburban developments around the outskirts of the city. Not far from the city centre, at the foot of Black Mountain, are the Australian National Botanic Gardens, which contain a comprehensive collection of native plants. Atop Black Mountain the huge Telstra telecommunications tower provides a magnificent vantage point for viewing the city and the surrounding countryside.

A SUBTROPICAL CAPITAL

Brisbane, the capital of Queensland, is not a 'true' tropical city, but in many respects could easily pass for one. The archetypal suburban Brisbane house with its weatherboard construction sitting high off the ground on wooden stilt-like pillars, between which wooden lattice-work allows the free flow of cooling breezes, reflects the way the inhabitants have acclimatised to the summer humidity. Throughout the city and its suburbs is a profusion of jacarandas, poinsettias, frangipanis and other hot-climate plants which thrive through Brisbane's long, hot summer days and short, mild winters.

The picturesque city is built on both banks of the Brisbane River, a few kilometres inland from Moreton Bay. No fewer than seven bridges span this slow-flowing waterway which winds in loops around the tall buildings and riverside parklands. The most distinctive of these is the steel-spanned Story Bridge, against which the city's high-rise development forms an attractive backdrop, especially in the evening when the bridge is illuminated by thousands of electric bulbs.

Among Brisbane's most notable landmarks are the 1920s neoclassical City Hall with Corinthian columns and a 91-metre Italian Renaissance clock tower; the copper-domed sandstone Customs House set flush on the bank of the Brisbane River; the University of Queensland buildings at St Lucia; Old Government House located between the river and the Queensland Institute of Technology; and the gracious Parliament House. On the other side of the Brisbane River is the Queensland Cultural Centre, set within the South Bank complex. Formerly the site of Expo '88, it is now a sophisticated mixture of galleries, theatres, promenades and restaurants. Within the cultural centre are the city's art collection, the state library and museum, and a number of venues for the performing arts.

The city's Botanic Gardens date back to the mid-1880s and cover 20 hectares on the banks of the Brisbane River. They have been supplemented by the 57-hectare Mount Coot-tha Botanical Gardens which contain the largest subtropical displays of flora in Australia.

Above Brisbane's handsome Customs House, fronting the Brisbane River at Petrie Bight, dates from 1889. With its solid Corinthian columns, twin pediments and elegant copper dome, it is one of several fine neoclassical buildings that were built in the city towards the end of the 19th century. *Left* The city's subtropical climate of long, warm, humid summers and short, mild winters has given rise to a distinctive form of domestic architecture. Made of timber and circled by wide verandas, these houses are built off the ground to catch cool breezes beneath the floorboards.

Above The Victoria Bridge sweeps across the gently flowing Brisbane River, linking South Brisbane with the city's central business district.
Right The Mount Coot-tha Botanic Gardens to the west of the city house many exotic and native plants. The distinctive domed glasshouses of the gardens protect and nurture an impressive collection of tropical vegetation.
Below Completed in 1940, the Story Bridge was designed by Dr John Bradfield, the engineer who also designed Sydney's Harbour Bridge. The central span of the graceful cantilevered structure is some 300 metres long.

THE BIENNIAL ADELAIDE FESTIVAL OF ARTS

On the evening of 11 March 1960, about 150 000 people thronged the streets of Adelaide to watch a festive torchlight parade of decorated floats and brass bands. It was the prelude to the opening, the following day, of the first Adelaide Festival of Arts – two jam-packed weeks of concerts, plays, operas, art exhibitions, poetry readings and literary forums.

Among the many celebrated artists who performed at this inaugural festival were the great American jazz pianist Dave Brubeck, the British Shakespearian actor Sir Donald Wolfit, the Australian conductor Charles Mackerras and the Australian soprano Joan Hammond who starred in the first Australian production of Richard Strauss's opera Salome. The highlight of the festival was a performance of T.S. Eliot's Murder in the Cathedral.

The festival was the brainchild of John Bishop, director of the Elder Conservatorium, and Sir Lloyd Dumas, chairman of Adelaide's Advertiser newspaper. They had long entertained the vision of a cultural festival similar to Scotland's Edinburgh Festival and during the 1950s they successfully lobbied local businessmen for financial support.

The buildings that now house most of the festival performances were completed between 1973 and 1977. They comprise the white-roofed Festival Theatre, which is both a concert hall and a venue for opera; the Playhouse, which seats more than 600 people; the Space, which is dedicated to experimental theatre; and the Amphitheatre, whose tiered seats and surrounding walkways can seat over 1000 people.

THE FESTIVAL CITY

Adelaide, the capital of South Australia, was built to a simple but highly practical design. Drawn up in 1837 by South Australia's first Surveyor General, Colonel William Light, the city was developed for free settlers; it is the only Australian state capital never to have received transported convicts. Every two years the city plays host to the Adelaide Festival of Arts, one of the world's most significant gatherings associated with performing arts and literature. The focal point of the festival is the Adelaide Arts Centre, which opened in 1973 in a picturesque parkland setting on the banks of the Torrens River on the northern edge of the city centre. Immediately south of the Arts Centre is the late 19th-century Parliament House, and across the river to the north is the Adelaide Oval which, with its riverside location, is often described as one of the world's most attractive sporting locations.

Compared with its eastern mainland counterparts, Adelaide is a small city with only modest high-rise development in its commercial sector. To the north, the foothills of the Mount Lofty Ranges form an attractive backdrop. Only 5 kilometres from the city is the Southern Ocean which provides Adelaide with welcome cool breezes on hot days. A tram service, the only one remaining in the state, connects the city with the historic beach suburb of Glenelg.

Opposite The white geometric roof of the Adelaide Arts Centre on the Torrens River, the venue for the city's annual international arts festival.
Below South Australia's first white settlers came ashore here at Glenelg, now the terminus of the Adelaide tramline, the only one in the state.

Above The lookout point on Montefiore Hill to the north of Adelaide provides panoramic views across green parklands of the city skyline.
Below Rundle Street is one of Adelaide's favourite shopping precincts. Particularly popular with locals are the outdoor cafes of East End.

THE SUNNIEST CAPITAL

Despite its physical isolation from the other large cities – Adelaide is the nearest capital city, more than 2000 kilometres away – Perth's enticing climate, picturesque setting on the banks of the Swan River and rapid commercial and cultural development during recent years have made it one of the county's fastest growing capital cities. A minerals boom in Western Australia during the 1970s spawned a rush of development which saw a major transformation of the city centre and a rapid rise in its skyline. Much of historic Perth was lost in the headlong rush to rebuild but several buildings, including a courthouse built in 1836, just seven years after the founding of the settlement, remain intact. The port town of Fremantle, 18 kilometres to the south-west and now part of Perth's metropolitan area, has retained more of its history. There are numerous relics of the brief period between 1850 and 1869 when convicts were transported to Western Australia, as well as the grim Round House, Western Australia's first gaol, which opened for business in January 1831.

Perth receives more sunshine than any other Australian capital and its inhabitants are devotees of sun, surf and the broad estuary of the Swan River. On any summer weekend it becomes a blaze of brilliant colour and activity as all manner of pleasure craft and racing yachts compete for space on its placid waters. A grand view of the city and its aquatic playground can be seen from the sweeping expanse of Kings Park. From this elevated stretch of natural bushland, where every spring masses of wildflowers burst into vibrant colour, one can see the curve of the estuary and the soaring skyscrapers that line St Georges Terrace, the city's principal commercial centre.

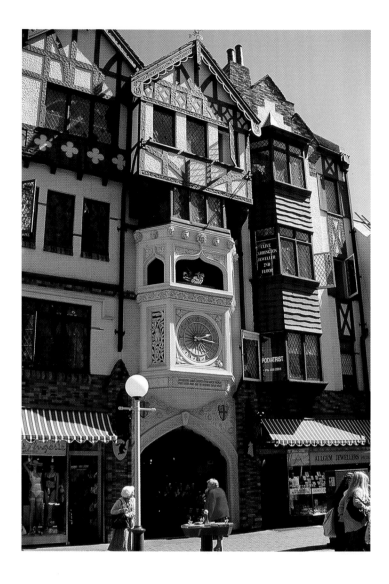

Above right *The London Court shopping arcade has a mock Tudor frontage and features models of St George and the Dragon, among others.* ***Below*** *Fremantle's Round House, Western Australia's oldest building, once housed over 100 prisoners within eight very small and depressing cells.*

Opposite *Perth's modern skyline looms above the graceful Swan River, the modern glass and steel buildings glinting in the last of the afternoon's sun.* ***Below*** *Kings Park, to the south of Perth, covers 400 hectares and is a blaze of riotous colour as fields of wildflowers bloom in the spring.*

A LIVING MUSEUM

Hobart is Australia's smallest state capital and, by general consensus, its most picturesque. The lack of rapid development that has been a feature of most of the mainland capitals has left Hobart without significant high-rise buildings but with a wealth of historical monuments and buildings intact. These heritage sites make Tasmania's capital a living museum of the colonial past. But the city's charm derives first and foremost from its marvellous setting between the brooding mass of Mount Wellington to the city's west and the gentle waters of the Derwent River, which defines the eastern boundary of the city's commercial centre.

Hobart is best viewed from the water except, perhaps, for the panoramic vistas of the town and its surrounds which can be enjoyed from the summit of Mount Wellington. The sight of the town against its mountain backdrop delights many a weary sailor as the entrants in the famous Sydney–Hobart Ocean Yacht Race sail up the Derwent every year in late December to their destination in Sullivans Cove. Surrounding and adjacent to this dockside area are a number of handsome sandstone buildings, including a string of old warehouses (many of them now given over to restaurants, galleries and shops), the stately Parliament House built in the 1830s, and the beautiful Customs House of 1802. To the south of Sullivans Cove is the historic precinct of Battery Point, dominated by the tower of St George's Anglican church. Other attractions include the castle-like Cascade Brewery, dating back to 1832, in the city's south-west environs, and the Wrest Point Hotel–Casino, which was Australia's first legal casino when it opened in 1973 on a prestigious riverside location.

Left *The lookout at the summit of Mount Wellington, a dormant volcano, allows spectacular views over Hobart and the Derwent River estuary.*
Below *Home to Hobart's fishing fleet, Victoria's Dock is usually quiet but comes alive during the Sydney–Hobart Ocean Yacht Race celebrations.*

Above *Resembling a European castle, the Cascade Brewery at the foot of Mount Wellington brews a quality beer that enjoys popularity everywhere.*
Right *Port Arthur, a notorious place of cruel punishment for almost 50 years, holds powerful memories of Tasmania's early history.*
Below *South of Hobart at Port Arthur stand the ruins of an unnamed church, one of the sandstone structures remaining from the penal colony.*

DARWIN'S WORLD WAR II BOMBINGS AND CYCLONE TRACY

At 9.30 a.m. on 19 February 1942, just four days after the fall of Singapore, Darwin's town and harbour came under sustained attack from 188 Japanese bombers. The assault was completely un-expected and the people of Darwin were thoroughly unprepared for the devastation that was wrought. In fact, when a warning was radioed from a missionary on nearby Bathurst Island, the authorities assumed that the approaching planes belonged to the United States. As a result, warning sirens had been sounding for less than one minute when the first bombs fell. In about an hour, eight ships in the harbour had sunk and about 150 crewmen were killed. The town was extensively damaged. Just over two hours later, 54 Japanese bombers shelled the airforce base, wrecking 20 Australian as well as several United States aircraft. Over 240 people died in these attacks and about 400 were injured, although official reports at the time put the death toll at only 17.

Almost 23 years later, in the dark early hours of Christmas Day 1974, a second destructive force caught the town of Darwin by surprise. Cyclone Tracy, with winds of up to 217 kilometres per hour, ripped the town apart, crushing many of its flimsy timber structures and hurling roofs, telephone boxes, trees, and even cars through the air. Sixty-six people died, 1000 were injured and more than half the town's population of about 48 000 was made homeless in the three hours during which the storm raged.

GATEWAY TO THE NORTH

Darwin in the north-west of the Northern Territory is Australia's only tropical capital, and is a town whose relaxed ambience and handsome, functional, contemporary buildings belie its turbulent history. Darwin has twice been destroyed: in 1942, during World War II, it was subjected to no fewer than 64 air raids; and on Christmas Eve in 1974 it was devastated by Cyclone Tracy, which left almost none of the city's buildings standing. One of the few buildings to survive both catastrophes is the fine seven-gabled Administrator's House which overlooks the harbour in the town's south-east. The most conspicuous reminders of Cyclone Tracy are the exhibits, including photographs and films, that are on display in the old Fannie Bay Gaol.

A fear of cyclones has not prevented Darwin's rapid expansion as a tourist centre. Tourism now ranks second only to mining as a contributor to the local economy. Besides the attraction of Diamond Beach Casino, Darwin provides convenient access to Kakadu National Park, Katherine Gorge and the many other prime destinations in the Top End. The early evening markets at Mindil Beach offer a unique opportunity to savour an exotic range of Asian foods, to observe the great racial diversity that characterises modern Darwin – Chinese, Aborigines and people from all parts of South-East Asia form part of the ethnic mix – and to enjoy one of Fannie Bay's wonderful sunsets.

Above Australian-style hats are among the many temptations on offer at the vibrant sunset markets held in the park behind Mindil Beach.
Opposite The 1883 Palmerston Town Hall fell victim to Cyclone Tracy in 1974, one of three cyclones that have devastated the city over the years.
Below One of the highlights of any visit to Darwin in the Northern Territory is the experience of watching a tropical sunset over Fannie Bay.

THE

ARID

CENTRE

THE ARID CENTRE

he 'red centre', 'dead heart', 'arid interior' – these expressions are commonly used to characterise the arid and semi-arid core of Australia's vast outback. In a sense, however, these are misnomers, because desert and semi-desert areas cover the greatest part of the continent and, in much of the west, extend right to the coast. More than two-thirds of the area of Western Australia, which itself covers a third of mainland Australia, is desert, while the vast, flat Nullarbor Plain stretches right across most of the southern coastline of South Australia and Western Australia. Even in the east, the really fertile areas are restricted mainly to the coastal belt, the limits of which are defined by the Great Dividing Range. Once the western slopes of these mountains have been left behind, the country flattens out, the rainfall becomes less reliable, and the vegetation becomes sparser until the landscape becomes what explorer Charles Sturt described as an expanse of 'gloomy scrub that extended like a sea to the very horizon' before merging into arid desert.

Yet this image of unmitigated barrenness does not do justice to the considerable variety of Australia's arid regions, or to their often sombre beauty. The word 'desert' conjures up visions of flat stretches, unrelieved by vegetation and unyielding in their harshness. This description does encompass some regions of the continent, most notably the so-called gibber deserts where the plains are covered with round rocks known as gibbers (from an Aboriginal word, 'giba', meaning stone), and where almost nothing grows and very little wildlife exists. Gibber plains are scattered throughout the centre, sometimes alternating with sandy stretches, and at other times occurring in unbroken expanses. In total, they cover about one-third of the desert regions. The most famous of these is Sturts Stony Desert, located in the north-east corner of South Australia. The hapless explorer, Charles Sturt, often regarded as the father of Australian exploration, encountered this desert in 1845 during his futile search for an inland sea and described it as 'the gateway to hell', where there grew 'not a blade of anything for our horses' whose hooves were torn and punctured by the sharp-edged stones. The gibber plains undoubtedly represent the harshest and most uncompromising face of Australia's outback.

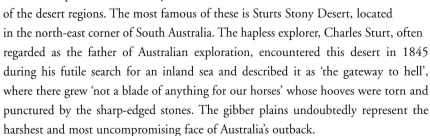

Previous pages Endless red dunes surround Cordillo Downs in north-east South Australia.
Previous pages (inset) Uluru rises dramatically out of a flat landscape dotted with shrubs.
Opposite The Bungle Bungles consist of weathered, contoured hills carved out of sandstone.

Of the sandy deserts, the Simpson Desert, which covers a vast 150 000 square kilometres of south-west Queensland, north-east South Australia and the south-east corner of the Northern Territory, is the most consistently severe. Huge sand ridges, which vary in colour from almost pure white to a deep orange-red and are up to 20 metres high, run in parallel lines which are sometimes unbroken for up to 80 kilometres. Between these dunes, in 200-metre-wide valleys, a scrubby vegetation grows and thrives. The ubiquitous spiky spinifex grass and ground-hugging saltbushes are the most prominent plants, while along the few, usually dry watercourses which traverse this region grow coolibah trees, the most familiar eucalyptus species of inland regions. Even the dunes are colonised in places by patches of spinifex, cane grass and bushy daisy. After summer rain – the Simpson Desert receives a meagre 150 millimetres each year – both the dunes and the valleys will burst briefly into colour as the dormant seeds, nourished by the moisture, sprout and bloom.

Left Hot-air ballooning is popular with visitors to Alice Springs, offering an adventure as well as marvellous views of the surrounding desertscapes. Below Even in the arid outback, masses of wildflowers periodically burst from the dunes after a healthy downpour of rain. These blooms cover the deserts near Innamincka, close to the Queensland–South Australia border.

ANIMAL ADAPTATIONS

Native animal life, too, increases markedly after rain. Birds are the most prolific and conspicuous, and include falcons, galahs and a range of honeyeaters. Even in the driest times the Simpson and the other sandy deserts support a surprisingly wide range of wildlife. A number of small mammals have adapted to life in these arid conditions by spending the heat of the day in cool underground burrows or in cracks in the earth. Because of their size and their subterranean lifestyle, many of them are rarely seen. One of the most unusual is the eyeless marsupial mole, which slithers along beneath the sand, feeding on insects and beetle larvae and rarely surfacing. Some animals, such as the tiny spinifex hopping-mouse, can survive without water. The spinifex hopping-mouse obtains the moisture it needs from the spinifex seeds on which it feeds. Of the larger mammals one of

the most prominent is the euro, a kind of wallaby that likes to take shelter from the fierce heat of the day among rocky outcrops.

The deserts are home to a large range of reptiles; some of them, such as the armour-plated thorny devil, are grotesque in appearance but almost none of them are threatening to humans. They range from tiny geckos to the giant perentie, the world's second-largest lizard, which can grow to over 2 metres long. Many of these are brilliantly patterned in colours that allow them to blend almost imperceptibly into their surroundings. The water-holding frog is one animal that has adapted well to desert conditions. It remains burrowed beneath the sands during periods of drought, using water stored in its bladder and in glands beneath its skin. After rain, it emerges to replenish its water supply and to lay its eggs on the bottom of shallow pools.

Above The dog fence at Camerons Corner, which forms the junction between the borders of Queensland, South Australia and New South Wales, was constructed to prevent dingoes from entering pastoral land. *Below* Despite its threatening spines, the thorny devil is a harmless lizard.

Above Dingoes are common in the arid outback regions, yet very few of them have retained a pure bloodline since the arrival of domestic dogs. *Below* Usually found basking in the sun, the spectacularly adorned frilled lizard is one of the most commonly found reptiles in northern Australia.

WITHIN ROCKY CLEFTS

The flat plains that characterise much of the desert and semi-desert landscapes are relieved by a number of gaunt rocky ranges, worn-down remnants of once much higher and verdant mountains. The quartzite MacDonnell Ranges, which describe a 400-kilometre arc that stretches to the east and west of Alice Springs, are the longest and highest of these ranges, although after 350 million years of weathering and erosion they are a mere skeleton of their former height. These mountain ranges encompass a number of spectacular features, such as Standley Chasm, Simpsons Gap and Finke Gorge. Some contain permanent waterholes and very often sustain lush vegetation. In certain places tall river red gums grow proudly along the sandy beds of dried-up rivers and gather sustenance from the reserves of water that lurk beneath the ground. The most majestic of the MacDonnell Ranges' gorges is Ormiston Gorge, a vast natural amphitheatre walled

in by 300-metre-high cliffs, its base strewn with huge boulders. In parts of the gorge are impressive stands of river red gums, whose smooth white trunks and olive-green foliage contrast dramatically with the reddish ochre of the towering quartzite walls. Ormiston and the other gorges of the MacDonnells are also a habitat for a palm-like plant, the cycad. These dark green plants with large spreading fronds can live for up to 500 years and are rainforest relics – survivors of those ancient times when all of central Australia was covered with lush rainforest. Also noted for cycads and for its prolific vegetation is Kings Canyon further to the south in the George Gill Range. The deepest gorge in central Australia, its sheer sandstone cliffs tower over a luxuriant valley in which hundreds of species of trees and plants thrive around a deep and permanent waterhole. The peaceful beauty of this magnificent gorge has earned it the sobriquet 'The Garden of Eden'.

Above Ewaninga, south of Alice Springs, is the location of ancient Aboriginal rock carvings.
Opposite top Towering cliffs enclose Ormiston Gorge in the beautiful MacDonnell Ranges.
Opposite bottom Central Australia's Finke River is one of the world's oldest watercourses.
Following pages At Kings Canyon in the Northern Territory's Watarrka National Park, sheer terracotta-coloured sandstone cliffs plunge dramatically into a deep valley below.

Above A superb view awaits those who reach the lookout point above Serpentine Gorge on the western side of the MacDonnell Ranges.
Right The walls of Standley Chasm turn a dazzling orange when the sun passes overhead.

Above and opposite *Just over 100 kilometres south of Alice Springs is a magical place called Rainbow Valley where a sandstone bluff forms the backdrop to a vast claypan, which is usually dry. The late afternoon sun highlights a dramatic rocky outcrop jutting out of the sandstone cliffs.*

Below left *The 50-metre-high Chambers Pillar, located south of Rainbow Valley, is a lonely sandstone remnant of a once extensive range of hills.* **Below** *The limestone cliffs at Geikie Gorge in the West Kimberley were carved by the mighty waters of the Fitzroy River over millions of years.*

Above and below Uluru is best seen when it catches the glow from the last rays of the setting sun. The sandstone rock is so enormous that it dwarfs the vehicles belonging to visitors paying homage to the ethereal monolith.

ULURU—KATATJUTA

Looming out of the flat plain about 350 kilometres south-west of Alice Springs is the mighty sandstone mass of Uluru (or Ayers Rock as the explorer William Gosse named it in 1873). The monolith has become an icon for the Australian outback and is the country's most familiar natural symbol. Uluru is also a place of great spiritual significance for the Aboriginal people of the area; it is a source of Dreaming stories and the dwelling place of many of their ancestors. In recognition of its importance in Aboriginal life and ritual, the area containing Uluru and the wonderful collection of domed rocks about 40 kilometres to the west known collectively as Katatjuta (previously called the Olgas) came under the custodianship of the local Aboriginal community in 1985. This community now cares for and oversees operations within the Uluru–Katatjuta National Park where these symbolic and evocative natural monuments are located.

Uluru fascinates people both for its huge bulk – it is often claimed to be the world's largest monolith – and its form. The rock seems to

assume different characters when viewed from different vantage points, and in the course of the day can pass through a spectrum of colours ranging from delicate pink and rusty-brown to glowing copper-red and deep purple as the sun illuminates it from different angles and the vertical folds and channels that line its craggy face cast their shadows.

Katatjuta (its name means 'many heads'), with its series of huge rounded sandstone rocks enclosing mysterious ravines and wooded valleys, is also an inspiration to those who visit it. The first Europeans to see it were reminded of 'rounded minarets, gigantic cupolas and monstrous domes'. Comparing it with Uluru, explorer Ernest Giles pronounced Katatjuta 'more wonderful and grotesque' while Uluru was noted as being 'more ancient and sublime'.

About 100 kilometres south-east of Uluru, the flat-topped Mount Conner, 3 kilometres long and approximately 1 kilometre wide, rises almost 350 metres above the plain. Less spectacular than its more illustrious neighbours, but still impressive, Mount Conner is part of the same eroded sandstone mass. Some visitors mistake it for Uluru.

Above Although many visitors want to climb to the summit of Uluru, the Aboriginal custodians of the sacred rock frown upon the practice. Guided walks around the base of the rock provide equally impressive perspectives.

ULURU AND KATATJUTA

Traditionally, most non-Aboriginal Australians have known the two most distinctive rock formations in central Australia respectively as Ayers Rock and the Olgas, or Mount Olga. In 1872, the explorer Ernest Giles was the first European to see the great bulk of Uluru from the shores of Lake Amadeus. It was William Gosse, however, who first reached the rock the following year and who named it in honour of Sir Henry Ayers, the premier of the colony of South Australia. At that time the present Northern Territory was part of South Australia.

When Gosse arrived at Uluru in 1873, he was surprised to learn that Ernest Giles had already found it. It was Giles who named both Lake Amadeus, which he described as an 'infernal lake of mud and brine', and which had impeded his progress, and Mount Olga – the first after the king of Spain and the second after the king's wife, Olga. Mount Olga sub-sequently became known as 'The Olgas', because it consisted of a multiplicity of 'mounts', or domes.

In 1950 Ayers Rock, together with the area that immediately surrounds it, was declared a national park, and in 1958 this region was extended to include The Olgas. In 1977 the park was renamed the Uluru National Park in recognition of the Aboriginal name for Ayers Rock, meaning the 'great pebble'. The Aboriginal name Katatjuta, meaning 'many heads', is now commonly used to refer to Uluru's neighbour. In 1985 the Australian government returned Uluru to the Anangu people, its traditional Aboriginal owners.

Above and opposite *Katatjuta is a series of weathered domes that arise from the same sandstone massif as Uluru, which can be seen in the distance. Steep ravines wind their way between the rocks.*
Following pages *The Devils Marbles, huge granite boulders that were originally part of a single granite rock, are scattered on both sides of the highway to Alice Springs, south of Tennant Creek.*

LAKES OF SALT

In June 1840 the drover-turned-explorer, Edward John Eyre, struck out northwards from Adelaide in an attempt to push into the interior of the continent through the rugged Flinders Ranges. Barely two and a half months later, Eyre viewed from the top of the aptly named Mount Hopeless a seemingly endless series of dry salt-lake beds that blocked his progress and forced him to retrace his steps. The largest and most northerly of these lakes now bears his name.

Lake Eyre reaches its lowest point at 16 metres below sea level. It is both the lowest and, for most of the time, the driest point on the Australian continent. Lake Eyre is really two dry lakes separated by a narrow channel. Between them these lakes cover an area of 9000 square kilometres, a vast expanse of glistening white salt over a base of mud. In some places the salt is so thick that vehicles can be driven over it. In 1964 it became a centre of international attention when Sir Donald Campbell established a world speed record there.

On rare occasions – three or four times in a century – Lake Eyre attracts attention for another reason. At these times this desolate landscape becomes transformed into a veritable inland sea as floodwaters from Queensland's Channel Country flow along usually dry riverbeds that drain into Lake Eyre and fill it to a depth of about 3 metres. Then for a brief period, a mere couple of years, the area explodes with wildlife as ducks, pelicans, swans and a host of other waterbirds attracted by the fish washed down by the rivers arrive in great flocks, and kangaroos, emus, wallabies and other mammals come to its shores. Later, as the water eventually begins to subside and becomes progressively saltier, the animal visitors depart, the water drains away and the scene reverts to its former eerie stillness. Seeing Lake Eyre in its usual dried-out state, it is hard to imagine that in the period when humans first inhabited the continent – and perhaps as recently as 20 000 years ago – Lake Eyre was a vast freshwater lake with very deep waters that supported a flourishing marine life and luxuriant surrounds that nourished an interesting array of land animals.

Opposite It is hard to imagine that Lake Eyre, usually a dry, desolate and eerie landscape, once provided a watery haven for a variety of wildlife. *Below* Lying to the south of the vast Lake Eyre in the desert region of South Australia is Lake Torrens, one of Australia's largest saltwater lakes.

DONALD CAMPBELL'S
SPEED RECORD

In 1964, English speed driver Donald Campbell achieved his two greatest triumphs: he broke both the world land and water speed records, and became the only person ever to achieve both feats in the same year. He was also the first person to hold both records at the same time. On 17 July of that year Campbell drove Bluebird, *his sleek blue racing car powered by a Bristol Siddely Proteus 755 gas turbine engine, across the flat, salt-encrusted bed of Lake Eyre at a speed of 652.5 kilometres per hour.*

The record he broke was held by another English speedster, Malcolm Campbell, who in September 1935 had achieved a speed of just over 485 kilometres per hour. He was also driving a car called Bluebird, *and his record was also set on a salt surface – on the Bonneville Salt Flats in Utah.*

On the very last day of 1964, Donald Campbell, this time in a boat called Bluebird, *sped across Lake Dumbleyung in Western Australia at 444.71 kilometres per hour, breaking the old record of 420 kilometres per hour that he had set in England in May 1959.*

Campbell's record-breaking car, which was built at a cost of a million pounds, had its first trial run in July 1960. Barely two months later he survived a crash at over 560 kilometres an hour, which left Bluebird *severely damaged. His luck eventually ran out in January 1967; he was killed when his boat* Bluebird *somersaulted as he attempted to break his water speed record on Coniston Water in Lancashire, England.*

LAKES OF SAND

In the south-west of New South Wales, 250 kilometres south-east of Broken Hill, is a landscape of dried-out lake beds and dunes sculpted by the elements into shapes of surreal beauty. The Willandra Lakes, as they are collectively known, is also a place of enormous archaeological significance – a veritable treasure house of clues to ancient human and natural history. Between about 40 000 and 18 000 years ago, these sandy depressions, in some places covered with saltbush, spiky grasses and straggling multi-stemmed mallee and bordered by extensive semi-circular sand dunes, or lunettes, were filled with fresh water that created a home for mussels, golden perch and Murray cod. They were filled by the now dry Willandra Creek, which once carried water from the Lachlan River further to the east. The entire lake system has been listed as a World Heritage site. The largest one is Lake Mungo, and along its eastern shore for more than 30 kilometres runs the spectacularly moulded white lunette known as the Walls of China – probably named by Chinese who worked on nearby Gol Gol sheep station in the 19th century. In the 1960s, important archaeological finds were made at Mungo. These included cremated human remains dating back 30 000 years – the oldest human remains ever found in Australia and the oldest evidence of cremation found anywhere in the world.

Until 1978 much of the Willandra Lakes region was occupied by an extensive sheep station, Mungo Station, the successor of Gol Gol Station. The station was then purchased by the New South Wales National Parks which established a 28 000-hectare protected area known as the Mungo National Park. Since grazing has ended, much of the region's natural vegetation has returned, as have most of the animals that inhabit semi-arid mallee country, such as emus.

Right *The Walls of China are spectacularly eroded lunettes that follow Lake Mungo's northern and eastern shores in the Mungo National Park.*
Below *Relics from the former Mungo Woolshed, which operated for more than a century as a sheep station, still remain in Mungo National Park.*

ISLANDS,

REEFS AND

COASTLINES

ISLANDS, REEFS

AND COASTLINES

*M*ost Australians live and earn their livelihood in the large cities along the continent's eastern seaboard. The Pacific coast also beckons them as a place of pleasure and recreation. Along most of its length, and especially between southern New South Wales and central Queensland, there is a string of seaside resorts, many with surfing beaches and others in sheltered bays, that attract holiday-makers all year round. The coast, even more than the countryside, is a place to get away from it all, and to own a 'weekender', or holiday home, on the coast is an ambition dear to the hearts of city dwellers. The lure of the seaside never seems to diminish. Holiday destinations such as Port Macquarie, Coffs Harbour and Byron Bay in New South Wales, and Queensland's Gold and Sunshine coasts to the south and north of Brisbane respectively, are popular with young and old. Many senior citizens decide that their years of labour have finally earned them a place in the sun as they eagerly seek to retire near the water.

AN INCREDIBLE REEF

Situated off the coast of tropical Queensland, stretching for more than 2000 kilometres from beyond the tip of Cape York south to the waters near Bundaberg, runs the Great Barrier Reef, one of the world's richest and most prolific marine environments and, by general consensus, Australia's greatest natural wonder. The World Heritage-protected Great Barrier Reef is contained within the Great Barrier Reef Marine Park and is an extremely intricate system – a giant living organism. It consists of more than 3000 individual coral reefs that range in area from less than 1 hectare to well over 100 square kilometres. In some places these reefs are very close to the coast and they also fringe some of the islands that are scattered like jewels in the ocean. In the more southerly section they lie up to 150 kilometres out to sea. The multi-hued collection of corals that form these reefs are sometimes described poetically as exotic underwater gardens filled with flowers that assume an incredible variety of fantastic shapes. These corals are represented by names such as staghorns, brains, feathers, fans and plates.

Previous pages A spectacular aerial perspective of Whitehaven Beach on Whitsunday Island.
Previous pages (inset) The Protector *was scuttled on Heron Island to provide a safe anchorage.*
Opposite High-rise apartments overlook the beachfront at Surfers Paradise on the Gold Coast.

Corals are not, in fact, flowers but vast colonies of tiny living animals called polyps. Each polyp secretes a tiny amount of limestone which binds the colonies together and forms the underlying structure of the reef. These beautiful fragile communities build slowly upwards and outwards, and can take many thousands of years to form. They continue to grow until they reach the surface of the water where exposure to the atmosphere kills them. Corals need warm water and sunlight in order to survive, and they therefore grow typically where the underlying seabed has built up to a few metres below the water surface. The reef outlines are clearly visible from the air, but to appreciate the wonderful variety of shapes and colours of the corals and of the 1500 or so species of fish that inhabit this environment, it is necessary to view them at closer quarters through a glass-bottomed boat, by snorkelling directly above them, or by getting even closer and scuba diving. Always remember, though, that corals are extremely fragile and take a long time to form so be careful not to damage them.

Above A spectacular aerial view of the Great Barrier Reef shows the vast extent and complex nature of the structure. Like an intricate root system, the reefs spread out in tortuous patterns. Varying water depths create the subtle gradations in colour. What is clearly visible from above is often not evident at sea level, and it is easy to appreciate the difficulty that ships have experienced in navigating this hazardous waterway.

Below Intricately patterned gorgonian fan corals grow predominantly in the deep waters of the Great Barrier Reef, accessible only to scuba divers.

Opposite A diver pauses to examine a sea whip coral, the large tentacles of which extend into the current to capture passing particles of food.

ISLANDS OF CORAL

There are about 250 islands within the Great Barrier Reef Marine Park, some of them tiny sand-covered coral cays, others substantial and lushly vegetated continental islands; many are surrounded by extensive fringing reefs. Coral cays are products of the reef, forming when a piece of reef becomes exposed and begins to accumulate sand, coral rubble and other debris. Many of these cays never develop beyond this stage but others slowly acquire a covering of vegetation and eventually become established islands as seeds and other nutrients are washed ashore by waves, blown in by the wind or dropped by birds. If you fly over the reef it is possible to see coral cays, often in close proximity to each other and in varying stages of development.

One of the most opulently vegetated coral cays is Green Island, just north of Cairns. At the island's resort, holiday-makers can safely observe two captive saltwater crocodiles and can stroll through well-developed forests, including a pocket of rainforest. Near the southern end of the Great Barrier Reef Marine Park is Heron Island, a coral cay named after one of the varieties of seabird that abound on the island. Lady Elliot and Lady Musgrave islands, two developed cays at the southern extremity of the reef, are frequented by vast flocks of seabirds and also provide rookeries for several species of large turtle.

Top left Green Island, a true coral cay with national park status lying off the coast of Cairns, is blanketed in lush tropical rainforest vegetation.
Top right Clear waters and a pristine beach are features of Heron Island, a vital turtle-nesting site at the southern end of the Great Barrier Reef.
Above left Like many of the other islands and coral cays, the economy of Dunk Island, north of Townsville, is based on its popularity as a resort.
Above right Accessible from the towns of Bundaberg and 1770 on the mainland, Lady Musgrave Island is a popular spot with keen snorkellers.
Opposite A metre-long green turtle slowly returns to the sea after laying her eggs on the sandy beach in the protected wilderness of Heron Island.

CONTINENTAL ISLANDS

Generally recognisable by their hilly terrain and densely wooded slopes, continental islands are the tips of submerged mountain ranges that once formed part of the mainland. One of the most glorious examples of these aptly named islands is the Whitsunday Group. The Whitsundays spread out along a 70-kilometre stretch between Mackay and Bowen and include some of the reef's most popular tourist resorts, such as Brampton, Hamilton, Hayman and Lindeman islands. On these enchanting tropical islands is a wide range of environments: sandy beaches, sheltered bays and spectacular hills, some covered with grassy slopes, others heavily wooded or dotted with rainforest patches. The largest and the most beautiful and varied of the continental islands along the Queensland coast is Hinchinbrook, north of Townsville. Separated from the mainland by a narrow channel, rich in marine and bird life, this island is dominated by a lofty, rugged range where the lush vegetation is broken only by steep, rocky cliffs.

Above Hamilton, one of the many continental islands in the Whitsunday Group, has a great tourist resort that allows easy access to natural settings.

AN ISLAND OF SAND

About 160 kilometres north of Brisbane is an island of a very different kind and a natural wonder in its own right. Fraser Island is the world's largest sand island and, along with the sand dunes of the adjacent coast, belongs to the Great Sandy National Park. Over 100 kilometres long, and at one point 25 kilometres wide, Fraser Island comprises a number of distinct environments. Parts of the island consist of extensive and shifting sand dunes and long stretches of pristine beaches, while in other places the dunes are covered with thick vegetation. In the north of the island is a series of cliffs where the sand, consolidated by clay and stained by minerals in shades ranging from black to golden brown, has been sculpted into shapes that both stimulate and challenge the imagination. Most remarkable of all, however, are the extensive stretches of rich subtropical rainforest that the island sustains and through which flow limpid streams over beds of pure sand. Dominating these rainforests are two conifers, the kauri pine and the satinay, a huge, rough-barked turpentine that can grow 50 metres tall and is found almost nowhere else in the world. The 40 perched lakes, trapped above sea level among the sand dunes scattered throughout the southern part of the island, are another unique feature. One of them, Lake Boomanjin, covers 200 hectares and is the largest perched dune lake in the world. Surrounded by scrubby vegetation, its waters are a reddish-brown, stained by leaf tannins and other decaying vegetable matter. At the other end of the spectrum, Lake McKenzie, surrounded by wooded hills and rimmed with a border of pure white sand, has clear, limpid waters.

Fraser Island and the coastal region are the habitat of many native birds, including the ground parrot, a flightless but fleet-footed avian that is rare elsewhere. Mammals are evident, with some bats and gliders feeding on the banksias that are prevalent in the area. The most conspicuous mammals are the 200 or so dingoes that live on the island and brumbies, or feral horses, descendants of the workhorses that were introduced to the island more than a century and a quarter ago. In the Great Sandy Strait, a narrow strait that separates Fraser Island from the coastal parts of the Great Sandy region, mangroves and extensive beds of seagrass sustain a varied marine fauna. Besides the many species of fish, dugongs, dolphins and turtles (similar to the turtles that inhabit the Great Barrier Reef) live in this strait.

Above and below *Fraser Island, off southern Queensland, is composed of sand formations in countless subtle shades from cream through to brown, evoking names such as The Cathedrals. Endless sandy beaches that run the length of the east coast often form cliffs, giant dunes and other shapes.*

Above A car ferry departs regularly for the sandy southern tip of Fraser Island from Inskip Point on the coast of Queensland near Noosa.
Right Lake Boomanjin, a vast and beautiful expanse of water above sea level on Fraser Island, is the highest perched dune lake in the world.

Above The deteriorating wreck of the trans-Tasman liner, Maheno, was blown onto the east coast of Fraser Island during a cyclone in 1935.
Below The crystal-clear waters of Fraser Island's Lake McKenzie are bordered by superb beaches and surrounded by majestic blackbutt forests.

DUGONGS' HABITAT AND FRAGILE HOLD ON LIFE

There are now only four surviving species of sea cow in the world. One is the dugong, which inhabits the warm waters around Australia's northern coasts and whose range extends from Vanuatu in the east along the coastlines of the Pacific Islands and Asia right across to the east coast of Africa. The other three remaining species are the manatees that occur in the Atlantic Ocean.

The dugong is a large, docile animal that grows to 3 metres long and often weighs as much as 500 kilograms. It is the world's only herbivorous marine mammal, and feeds exclusively off beds of seagrass that grow in shallow coastal waters. It is thought to have descended from the same ancient ancestors as the elephant but, unlike its distant terrestrial relative, it has spent its entire life in the water.

The dugong's nostrils are on top of its head and are covered with flaps while the animal is underwater. The flaps open when the animal's head is above water so that it can breathe. It propels itself through the water by moving its broad tail flukes up and down, using its small forelimbs to keep its body stable and to steer its course.

Once hunted commercially for their oil, dugongs are now a protected species in most countries. One factor that has influenced their endangered status is an extremely slow rate of reproduction; the female does not bear her first calf before the age of 10 years. A single young is born about a year after mating and it is suckled and carried around on its mother's back for up to 18 months.

AN UNMATCHED MARINE HABITAT

About 4000 kilometres away from the Great Barrier Reef, on the opposite side of the Australian continent but at almost the same latitude, is another favoured habitat for turtles, dolphins and dugongs. Shark Bay, on the coast of Western Australia and at the very edge of the western desert, is about as far south as dugongs, the world's only plant-eating marine mammals, occur. In fact, Shark Bay has the largest regular concentrations of dugongs anywhere in the world. They feed off the vast seagrass beds that grow there that cover more than one-eighth of the bay's total area. These beds, which are particularly profuse along the eastern side of the bay, also provide sustenance for large numbers of huge green and loggerhead turtles.

Shark Bay is a harsh desert-like environment, whose sandy shores are covered by low, scrubby vegetation. In spite of this, every July and August the area blooms with a magnificent and varied display of wildflowers, several species of which are found nowhere else. This extensive inlet on the Western Australian coast has an area of some 30 000 square kilometres, just over half of which is water. It is punctuated by the Peron Peninsula, which juts out into its centre.

The peninsula is the site of the first documented landing by a European on the Australian mainland – made by the Dutchman Dirck Hartog in 1616. Today it is famous for the dolphins that assemble at Monkey Mia on its eastern shores, to be hand-fed by human visitors. They are the world's only wild dolphins to have become so tolerant of human presence in their environment.

Hamelin Pool is an area in the south-east corner of Shark Bay where the water has an extremely high salt content. This occurs because the pool is protected from the tides by a sandbank and a bed of seagrass, and is subject to very high rates of evaporation. It provides an ideal environment for the survival and growth of stromatolites – ancient blue-green algae that first formed 3500 million years ago and that are joined together by sediment. One of the earth's oldest life forms, these stromatolites are alive and still growing, undisturbed by other forms of marine life which cannot tolerate the extreme salinity of the water. Their unusual shapes, which are formed by water currents, vary from large flat 'mats' to toadstool-shaped clubs and columns.

Three islands at the western extremity of the bay are important wildlife sanctuaries and provide habitats for some species that are very rare or non-existent elsewhere. The largest of the three, Dirk Hartog Island, has the only remaining populations of the white-winged fairy-wren, while the spinifex-covered Bernier and Dorre islands are the last refuge for a number of marsupials, including the western barred bandicoot and the western hare-wallaby.

Above left Stromatolites, ancient life forms, thrive in the saline waters of Hamelin Pool.
Above right The coastline around the town of Denham reveals Shark Bay's rugged beauty.
Left Eager tourists gather daily to meet and touch the bottlenose dolphins at Monkey Mia.
Right This dolphin sculpture at Monkey Mia is made from coquina, a hard substance that is formed from the shells of tiny marine molluscs.

SPECTACULAR CLIFFS

The Australian coastline is characterised by many long stretches of rocky cliff faces, but nowhere is the coast more dramatic than in the west. Running south from Dirk Hartog Island for 300 kilometres is a continuous line of brown limestone cliffs with a jagged appearance that is ample evidence of the fury of the Indian Ocean. Especially when viewed from the air, these eroded cliffs at the edge of a vast sandy plain present a vista of rugged grandeur.

The destructive power of the sea is also dramatically evident along the coastline of the Port Campbell National Park in southern Victoria. Here the violent waters of Bass Strait are eroding the soft limestone cliffs at a rapid rate, creating imposing natural sculptures as well as deep caves and gorges. Rising out of the water just near this coast, like a set of monstrous, misshapen teeth, are rock formations known as the Twelve Apostles. These are remnants of the coastal cliffs which have since receded. Just west of the Twelve Apostles stands what remains of a mighty formation known as London Bridge, a pair of arches jutting out into the sea from the cliff face. In 1990 the arch attached to the cliff collapsed, leaving the remaining arch stranded precariously in the sea, awaiting its turn to crumble.

Sailors in earlier days dubbed this coastline 'the shipwreck coast'. The most tragic wreck occurred in 1878 when an immigrant ship, the *Loch Ard*, ran ashore with the loss of 48 lives. The only two survivors, a boy and girl, both 18 years old, came ashore at the bottom of the cliffs in the inlet now known as Loch Ard Gorge. The ship's anchor was recovered and is now on display in the town of Port Campbell, the only calm and sheltered inlet along this treacherous coastline.

Above *The rugged southern Victorian coastline suffers the brunt of the stormy seas that roll in across Bass Strait, weathering the limestone rock.*
Right *The Twelve Apostles, a series of sea-sculpted offshore rocks in Port Campbell National Park, are accessible via Victoria's Great Ocean Road.*

Above and below *Loch Ard Gorge has a deceptively calm appearance, but dangerous, raging waters often flood into the narrow inlet. High cliffs, surmounted by coastal heath vegetation, line the entrance to the gorge.*
Opposite *London Bridge, a limestone rock formation that was once connected to the mainland along the Victorian coast, collapsed in 1990.*
Right *The Zuytdorp Cliffs, which bear the brunt of the mighty Indian Ocean, are part of an unbroken stretch of spectacular limestone cliffs that run for 300 kilometres south from Shark Bay in Western Australia.*

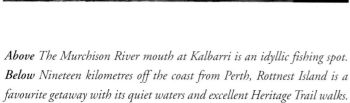

Above *The Murchison River mouth at Kalbarri is an idyllic fishing spot.*
Below *Nineteen kilometres off the coast from Perth, Rottnest Island is a favourite getaway with its quiet waters and excellent Heritage Trail walks.*

Above *Since 1896, the old lighthouse at Cape Leeuwin – a prominent headland at the extreme south-west tip of the Australian mainland – has marked the point where the mighty Indian and Southern oceans meet.*

Above *Wategos Beach at Byron Bay on the north coast of New South Wales is one of the finest surfing beaches on the eastern seaboard. Protected on the western side of Cape Byron, the beach faces north rather than east.*

Above *Known as the Remarkable Rocks, the huge granite boulders on an exposed headland on the western side of Kangaroo Island, off the coast of South Australia, have been shaped by centuries of wind and water erosion.*

Above *From the rocky foreshores at the tip of the wild and remote Cape York Peninsula, the most northerly point on the Australian mainland, tiny Yorke Island can be seen across a narrow strait. Although Cape York has always been home to Aboriginal people, today it is interesting to see that there are still numerous Aboriginal settlements at places such as Kowanyama and at Bamaga, which is almost at the tip of the peninsula.*

Left *Situated about 15 kilometres north of Cairns, on the so-called Marlin Coast, is the small settlement of Trinity Beach. With its golden palm-lined beach and lapping surf, it epitomises tropical tranquillity.*

Below *These dinghies on the beach at Seisia, near the township of Bamaga on the western side of the tip of Cape York Peninsula, come to shore from the Endeavour Strait. Across the strait, north-west from Seisia, is the small island known as Possession where in 1770 Captain James Cook proclaimed the eastern part of Australia as a British possession.*

LORD HOWE, A SOUTH SEA PARADISE

Rugged and rocky also describes the coastline of the extremities of Lord Howe Island, a horseshoe-shaped island set picturesquely in the Pacific Ocean almost 800 kilometres north-east of Sydney. Although it is so far off the coast, Lord Howe is officially part of the state of New South Wales and is one of Australia's prime tourist attractions, luring people both for its scenic beauty and its unique flora and fauna.

Lord Howe Island is a remnant of an ancient volcano and at the southern end of the island, the sides of two mountains, Mount Gower and Mount Lidgbird, display evidence of these volcanic origins. Even more dramatic evidence is provided just 3 kilometres to the south-east of the island where Balls Pyramid, a towering mass of volcanic rock, rises more than 550 metres out of the ocean.

The two arms of Lord Howe enclose a placid lagoon, protected by a 6-kilometre-long coral reef. This reef is the world's most southerly and sustains a rich variety of marine life, including many colourful corals. Lush rainforest vegetation abounds on the island; several species of palm and fern grow nowhere else and of the more than 200 species of flowering plant, about 60 are unique to the island.

Birds are perhaps the most spectacular of Lord Howe's fauna. The island can boast more than 120 species which either live there or visit regularly. In spring and summer the island is visited by huge colonies of seabirds which come to breed. In addition to having one of the largest breeding colonies of the spectacular red-tailed tropicbird, it is also the most southerly breeding place of the beautiful masked booby and the only remaining nesting place of the providence petrel. Lord Howe was once home to 14 species of land bird which had no natural predators until the arrival of humans in the last century. Since

then, the number has been reduced to only five. The rarest is the Lord Howe woodhen, a flightless bantam-sized bird which until recently was threatened with extinction. To protect the fragile environment of this jewel of the South Seas, the number of tourists permitted to stay on the island at any one time is strictly limited. To visit Lord Howe Island, then, is truly to escape 'far from the madding crowd' and to savour the relaxed ambience of one of nature's genuine masterpieces.

Above Pristine Lord Howe Island in the Pacific has a horseshoe-shaped lagoon that is enclosed by the world's most southerly living coral reef.
Below The attractive Lord Howe woodhen is endemic to the small island.
Opposite Like the rest of Lord Howe Island, and despite its forbidding, barren appearance, Balls Pyramid is home to many animals and plants.

MOUNTAINS

AND

FORESTS

MOUNTAINS AND
FORESTS

*A*ustralia is known as the flattest continent on earth. Its highest mountain, Mount Kosciuszko in the Australian Alps, is only 2228 metres above sea level and most of the old mountain ranges that are believed to have towered above this height have been worn down to mere shadows of their former selves. It is the continual reshaping of the rock formations, however, that creates the unique shapes that are synonymous with Australia.

The so-called mountain ranges of the centre and west of the continent are greatly eroded and often bare and rocky remnants of ancient mountains that were once densely wooded. Their very appearance is suggestive of their worn-down state. The mountains of the east, stretching continuously and never far from the coast, from near the tip of Cape York until they eventually merge into the flat country of western Victoria, are also weathered. The Great Dividing Range, despite the thick forests that cover most of its slopes, is itself in an advanced state of erosion. For millions of years rivers have gouged out deep chasms and the weather has worn down the peaks to produce mountain landscapes of rugged grandeur despite their size.

THE BLUE MOUNTAINS

Nowhere are chasms more spectacular than in the Blue Mountains, the most frequented parts of which lie west of Sydney. When Charles Darwin visited the region in 1836, he described the view across the Jamison Valley from near the present-day township of Wentworth Falls as 'most magnificent, astounding and unique' and the sheer sandstone walls that mark the contours of the deep valley as 'the most stupendous cliffs I have ever seen'. In fact the Jamison Valley is a huge canyon, smaller than the Grand Canyon, but much more ancient. A different perspective on this valley can be gained from various vantage points, but the most famous of all is the view from Echo Point near Katoomba, the largest town in the mountains and the valley's tourist and commercial centre. Here one can admire the Three Sisters, the most conspicuous of the many fantastic shapes into which the forces of nature have eroded pieces of exposed rock in different parts of the valley.

Previous pages The Three Sisters ascend near Katoomba in the majestic Blue Mountains.
Previous pages (inset) The north Queensland town of Ravenshoe is close to Millstream Falls.
Opposite Tamborine Mountain, near the Gold Coast, has panoramic views to both sides.

On the northern side of the Blue Mountain's narrow ridges, on which the settlements are built and along which the roads and railway tracks run to the west, is the Grose Valley, which can be best viewed from Govetts Leap near the township of Blackheath. Further to the west are the justly celebrated Jenolan Caves, a series of extensive underground caverns characterised by evocative limestone formations that have been carved out of the porous rock over many centuries by streams created by the slow seepage of rainwater into the caves.

Above *The aptly named Valley of the Waters near Wentworth Falls in the Blue Mountains contains many lovely waterfalls cascading into inviting pools that are surrounded by shady forest ferns and stately old gum trees.* **Left** *Sheer sandstone cliffs enclose the vast and imposing Grose Valley, one of the major canyons in the Blue Mountains. The best vantage point for this impressive vision is from well-known Evans Lookout at Blackheath.*

THE GRAMPIANS

Near the southern end of the Great Dividing Range in Victoria are the Grampians, named by the explorer Sir Thomas Mitchell after a range in Scotland and reminiscent, especially in wintry mists, of parts of the Scottish highlands. Like the Blue Mountains, the Grampians are characterised by deep chasms carved out among sandstone cliffs over which plunge spectacular waterfalls. Declared a national park in 1984, the area is a haven for wildlife and contains over 200 species of native birds, including emus, eagles and a variety of waterfowl.

Above The Grampians National Park is characterised by rocky overhangs and shelters, including this protruding slab known as The Balconies.
Below From the rocky outcrop at Reid Lookout, hikers can enjoy the expansive views across to Victoria's majestic Grampians National Park.
Opposite top The MacKenzie River plunges over the escarpment edge into a gorge of the same name in a succession of four breathtaking waterfalls.
Opposite bottom Cooler weather in autumn transforms the foliage near Hall's Gap in the Grampians from the usual green to warm mellow tints.

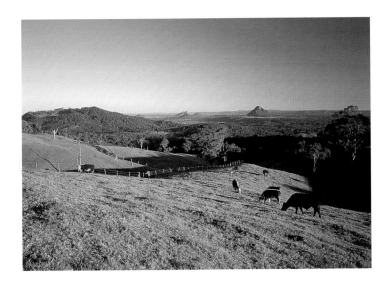

VOLCANIC REMNANTS

Further to the north-west, near the small town of Coonabarabran in central-western New South Wales, is a remarkable mountain range. The Warrumbungles' wooded hills and slopes are dramatically punctuated by uplifted remnants of volcanic rock in a bewildering array of shapes and formations that have been given such names as Belougery Spire, Crater Bluff and the Needle. The most arresting of these natural forms is the long, vertical, sharp-edged rock, dubbed the Breadknife, that juts almost 100 metres skywards from a narrow ridge.

In 1818 the explorer John Oxley, on seeing the Warrumbungles rising from the plain, enthused about this 'stupendous range of mountains...' with 'lofty hills arising from the midst of lesser elevations, their summits crowned with perpendicular rocks, in every variety of shape and form, that the wildest imagination could paint'. He decided to name them the Arbuthnot Range after a British official. The Warrumbungles' present and more appropriate name is from the local Aboriginal word which means 'crooked mountain'.

Above The Breadknife, a vertical sharp-edged rock in the Warrumbungles National Park, is just one of many unusual volcanic features in the area.
Top left The Glasshouse Mountains are a series of volcanic plugs that rise out of the surrounding pasture land on south-east Queensland's coast.
Left Mount Warning in far north-eastern New South Wales, a remnant of an eroded volcano, now rises to less than half its original height.
Opposite A total of 13 volcanic plugs, or mountain peaks, make up the Glasshouse Mountains, although only one can be climbed by fit hikers.

109

ALPINE SPLENDOUR

Beginning west of Canberra and stretching 400 kilometres to the south and south-east are the Australian Alps, the highest section of the Great Dividing Range. In winter the upper slopes of these mountains are covered in snow for a few months while the higher peaks retain their white blanket for a little longer. Some may find the term 'alps' an inappropriate one for mountains that have no permanent snow cover and whose high rocky plateaus are covered in summer with grasses and extensive patches of wildflowers. But in winter skiers flock to the numerous ski resorts in southern New South Wales and northern Victoria. At this time these mountains do take on a genuine alpine splendour that belies their modest elevation.

At the lower levels, the thickly wooded slopes contain a greater variety of eucalyptus species than any other part of the country and form one of the world's largest continuous expanses of forest. At higher altitudes hardier species, such as the tall and slender alpine ash and mountain gums, replace the candlebarks and stringybarks that predominate further down. Above 1500 metres, however, is the domain of the snow gum, which is itself a miracle of adaptation.

In the lower parts of its range it can stand tall and proud, supporting a mass of spreading branches. At the upper extremity, close to 2000 metres, it is gaunt and stunted, its trunk and branches twisted into weird shapes by the glacial conditions. Above about 1800 metres, there are virtually no other trees. The high slopes and plateaus, when they are not snow-covered, can sustain only ground-hugging grasses and bushes, as well as a spectacular array of pretty wildflowers.

Above left *Perisher Valley's ski slopes and snowfields in the Kosciuszko National Park are dotted with snow gums, a hardy alpine eucalypt.*
Above right *There are many ski resorts attracting enthusiastic skiers in the Kosciuszko National Park, including Smiggin Holes near Perisher Valley.*
Below left *A wide range of eucalypts grow abundantly on the forested slopes.*
Below right *Starting in the upper reaches of the alpine slopes, the Snowy River meanders downhill and passes the entrance to the national park.*
Opposite *During winter, Australians flock to Perisher Valley to make the most of the snow; in summer, they come to wander on the alpine heaths.*

TASMANIA'S HIGHLANDS

For many visitors to Tasmania, the strongest memory is of rolling hills and gentle valleys with picturesque farmlands covering the slopes. Although much of Tasmania's cultivated landscape is reminiscent of parts of the English countryside, the centre and the south-west corner of the island are places of wild and primitive beauty. It is a strange paradox that while the Australian mainland is the flattest continent, Tasmania has been described as the world's most mountainous island. Much of the centre of the island is occupied by the extensive Central Plateau with jagged dolerite cliffs and peaks – the product of ancient volcanic upheavals and the inexorable progress of glaciers – that create Australia's most awe-inspiring alpine vistas. Perched within this craggy landscape are several thousand elevated lakes, ranging from mere large ponds to expanses several kilometres long whose limpid cold waters reflect the sombre grey cliffs or snow-covered peaks that tower above them or, in some areas, the eucalypt forests that fringe their shores. Much of this region is contained in the vast Cradle Mountain–Lake St Clair National Park where the established Overland Track, which runs for more than 80 kilometres long, takes hikers through the region's most breathtaking scenery.

Left Soaring more than 1500 metres above sea level, the gaunt twin dolerite peaks of Cradle Mountain lie at the northern end of the Cradle Mountain–Lake St Clair National Park in the island state of Tasmania. *Below* Crater Lake is one of the many elevated lakes within the Cradle Mountain–Lake St Clair National Park. Rocks, or moraines, deposited by ancient glaciers, prevent the waters from escaping into the gorges below.

Above *The south-west of Tasmania has huge mountain ranges that have been eroded by the slow, unalterable movement of glaciers, leaving wide valleys and jagged peaks and ridges.*

Left *From the south-western highlands, the Gordon River has forged its way to the coast, completing its 180-kilometre journey at Macquarie Harbour. In one place, it flows through slopes covered with lush rainforest.*

Right *The white quartzite face of Frenchmans Cap, which is located just north of Macquarie Harbour, rises 600 metres from its base.*

Opposite *Red-necked wallabies are abundant in the open woodland areas of Tasmania. Like many Australian marsupials, the species has adapted well to the rugged island's climate.*

THE ORIGINS OF FIRE

There are numerous Aboriginal Dreaming stories about the origin of fire. One such story told by the Kulin people of Victoria pinpoints a specific feature of the landscape found in the Dandenong Ranges just east of Melbourne, at the southern extremity of the Great Dividing Range, where fire was believed to have originated.

According to their legend, at one time only one person, a woman named Kar-ak-ar-ook, possessed fire. She kept it in a special stick and used it to cook yams. One day a crow called Waung devised a plan to steal the fire. He hid some snakes under an anthill and then advised Kar-ak-ar-ook to dig out the ants' eggs with her magic stick. When Kar-ak-ar-ook saw the snakes, she beat them vigorously with her stick. Some of her fire fell on the ground, whereupon Waung grabbed it and flew off to the top of a tree, refusing to share it with anybody else.

Pund-jel, one of the spirits of the sky, decided to punish Waung's selfishness. He gathered some people together and they stood at the bottom of the tree and demanded the fire. Waung became frightened and threw down some fire with which the people set alight the dry grass. The surrounding country was soon aflame. Waung and two of Pund-jel's men were burnt by the fire; the scorched bodies of the two men were later transformed into the two large rocks at the bottom of the Dandenong Ranges. Kar-ak-ar-ook was also punished for her selfishness in keeping the magic of fire all to herself. Pund-jel banished her to the sky, where her stick still burns brightly among the other stars.

Above The enormous Gloucester Tree near Pemberton in Western Australia is used as a fire lookout.
Opposite bottom The Mulgrave River meanders through the bush near Gordonvale in Queensland.

A CANOPY OF BEAUTY

To enter a tropical or subtropical rainforest is to discover another world – one of eerie beauty. The first thing to strike the uninitiated visitor is the cathedral-like gloom of the place. What light there is, is filtered through an overarching canopy of leaves and branches, not unlike the soaring vaults of a Gothic nave. The canopy nearly or completely blocks out the sky and provides a cool respite from the humid tropical heat. The forest floor is covered with a mess of leaves and other fallen debris and at all levels there is a tangle of wild vegetation. A mass of ferns grows close to ground level, thick vines dangle from tree branches or wrap themselves around the trunks, and saplings struggle upwards in search of sunlight. Numerous epiphytes – palms, ferns and tree orchids – grow on these trunks, perched with seeming precariousness high off the ground. Many of the trees have massive trunks, buttressed by moss-covered roots that protrude above the earth. Here and there, trees have succumbed to invading strangler figs, twisting structures that can grow up to 45 metres tall with huge diameters. Many of these began life as tiny seeds on branches, sending out shoots which gradually engulfed and strangled their hosts.

Rainforests are a vastly shrunken, and ever shrinking, resource in Australia. This is the result both of natural climatic changes and of human intervention. Many early settlers in remote areas saw rainforest vegetation as an aberration, out of keeping with the continent's 'natural' sclerophyll vegetation. Impervious to their beauty, they logged many areas for building timber and cleared large areas for agriculture. The latter proved a largely fruitless pursuit as the lush growth of the rainforest covers poor, thin soils that are wholly unsuited to the growing of crops. Most of the nutrients on which rainforest plants survive are contained in the nourishing layers of leaf litter that collect on the floor of the forest.

The eucalypts, acacias and other hard-leafed sclerophyll plants that now characterise most of the Australian bush are descendants of the broader-leafed rainforest varieties that once covered much of the continent but which retracted towards the coastal fringes as weather patterns changed and the centre became drier. In the last 200 years the area of Australia covered by rainforest has been reduced by almost 75 per cent. Today, the remaining rainforests cover a total area of barely 20 000 square kilometres, much of it in small remnant patches and confined to coastal and mountain regions in the north and east.

Above left Forests thrive near Mount Beauty in north-western Victoria.
Above centre Mosses and ferns cover the rocky floor of Carnarvon Gorge.
Above right An imposing forest of stately trees skirts the tranquil waters of Lake Sanatorium in the Macedon Ranges National Park in Victoria.

THE DAINTREE

The Daintree National Park, about 80 kilometres north of Cairns on the far north Queensland coast, and the slightly more northerly Cape Tribulation National Park contain the greatest expanse of tropical rainforest in Australia. It is unique in that the rainforest of this region is not confined to the highlands but sweeps spectacularly right down to the coast. This area is part of a 500-kilometre-long strip between Townsville and Cooktown that has achieved World Heritage listing. Among the animals that are unique to this area are two species of tree kangaroo that have adapted to life high in the trees and a rare white possum, the lemuroid ringtail possum. Numerous bird species, too, are endemic to this region, including the beautiful golden bowerbird. Many species of colourful butterfly, among them the Cairns birdwing (the largest butterfly in Australia), can be seen flitting noiselessly through these forests, their colourful wings glinting in the patches of sunlight that pierce the thick forest canopy.

Australia's rainforests, and particularly those in the tropics, contain the country's greatest concentration of plant and animal species. Almost one-third of Australia's characteristic marsupials, nearly a quarter of all reptiles and one in every six native birds live in tropical rainforests. Many are found nowhere else. A high proportion of these animals live high in the canopy branches and never descend to the ground. Such reclusive lifestyles probably mean that many rainforest-dwelling animals have so far eluded human detection.

Right *Spectacular colours, especially the male's brilliant green and black wings, make the Cairns birdwing butterfly a truly distinctive species.*
Below *Panoramic views across the forests to the ocean can be enjoyed at the Mount Alexander Lookout in Cape Tribulation National Park.*
Opposite *A favourite pastime of visitors to north Queensland is the crocodile cruise along the Daintree River in the Daintree National Park.*

A VARIETY OF RAINFORESTS

The rainforests in the Daintree and nearby regions are the lushest, densest and most thickly canopied of all Australia's rainforests. Other rainforests in the tropics occur further north on Cape York, in Kakadu National Park, farther to the west in Arnhem Land and, in small patches, in parts of the Kimberley in the far north-west. These forests, often called monsoonal forests, have a more open and less elevated canopy and sparser vegetation than other tropical rainforests. This is because, in spite of the high overall rainfall, these areas experience a very long dry season – from May to October – and so are virtually drought-ridden for more than half the year.

In more southerly parts of the Great Dividing Range numerous areas of rainforest still survive. These vary in type from subtropical rainforests, which occur in patches throughout southern Queensland, New South Wales and even into parts of Victoria, through warm temperate rainforests, which are predominant in New South Wales, and cool temperate rainforests, which exist mainly in southern Victoria and western Tasmania. As we come down the scale from tropical to cool temperate, the forest types become less complex, the canopies lower and less enclosed and the number of dominant tree species fewer. The cooler forests are marked by a greater profusion of mosses and small ferns at ground level. Notable among the more southerly rainforests are the lush and extensive warm temperate forests in Washpool National Park in the New England district of northern New South Wales and a range of magnificent rainforest types in the spectacular Barrington Tops National Park in the upper Hunter Valley region of New South Wales.

Different kinds of non-eucalypts are the dominant, canopy-forming trees in the various types of rainforest. Conifers, especially the giant hoop pines, dominate many of the tropical rainforests of northern Queensland. At the other end of the spectrum in the cool temperate rainforests of south-west Tasmania, two other conifers are prominent, although their numbers have been greatly depleted as a result of logging. The Huon pine, which is related to the Canadian redwood, grows mainly in riverside locations. This slow-growing species can reach a height of 30 metres and often lives for more than 2000 years. Many stands of this noble tree were cut down and used to build boats. The King Billy pine, too, has been severely depleted, as it used to be in strong demand for furniture making.

Above right In the Barrington Tops National Park in New South Wales, dappled light filters through tree canopies onto the cool streams below.
Right In its lower reaches, Tasmania's Gordon River flows through thick forests, dressed here in their autumn foliage and reflected in the water.
Opposite Giant Huon pines, slow-growing conifers that are typically scruffy in appearance, grow near the Gordon River in Tasmania.

FORESTS OF THE FAR SOUTH-WEST

Most of Western Australia is arid and even in the south-west, rainfall is restricted mainly to the winter months. However, in a narrow strip along the far south-west coast, rain falls regularly all year round. The result of high rainfall is an area rich in eucalypt forests. Several species grow only in this region. In places with soil that is too poor to sustain other species, jarrah, a much sought-after hardwood species, often grows in pure stands. On richer soils, it shares the forests with another similar species, marri. In spring, the floor of jarrah forests comes alive with masses of colourful blooms. Both jarrah and marri regularly grow to 30 metres in height. Because of the jarrah's value as a hardwood building timber, forests of this particular eucalypt were until fairly recently in danger of extinction.

Another hardwood eucalypt species, which was once extensively logged for bridge construction, is the tuart, which can reach up to 40 metres in height and is thought to live for more than 300 years. It grows only on limestone soils and sometimes shares forests with jarrah and marri. The Tuart Forest National Park, a little north of the town of Busselton, however, covers almost 1800 hectares and is the last remaining forest of pure tuart.

But the grandest of all trees in the region, and one of the most majestic of all gums in Australia, is the white-trunked karri, which grows to more than 70 metres tall and is widespread throughout this south-west strip of Western Australia, particularly in the D'Entrecasteaux National Park. Because of its predominance, some parts of this coast are commonly referred to as the 'karri coast'.

Above *The slim white trunks of the majestic karri gums soar skywards.*
Right *A huge karri forest grows alongside the road to Augusta at the extreme south-western tip of Western Australia. In earlier times, Augusta flourished as a centre of the export trade in karri and other local timbers.*

AGRICULTURAL AND PASTORAL COUNTRY

AGRICULTURAL AND PASTORAL COUNTRY

*B*efore the arrival of Europeans, no form of agriculture seems to have taken place in Australia. The first crops were sown at Farm Cove where the Royal Botanic Garden in Sydney now stands. The crops failed and it wasn't until the colony pushed further west that land suitable for farming became available. Over the centuries the land has become an important source of economic revenue. In the coastal areas where sufficient rainfall and mild temperatures allow, food crops are grown. From northern New South Wales to north of Brisbane, sugar cane and other tropical fruit plantations are prolific. Wheat and sheep farming occur further inland and beef cattle are raised on the drier pastures of the interior.

EXPLOITING THE INTERIOR

Seen from the air, it looks like any other scrub-covered patch of arid central Australia, except that in the distance there is a square of bright green and a cluster of low-slung buildings. As the aircraft approaches them, the main building defines itself as a timber homestead, roofed in corrugated iron, with a generous shaded veranda. Immediately surrounding the homestead is a tended lawn, some flowering bushes and three or four tall trees. Beyond the house, scattered in a radius of several hundred metres, is an assortment of large and small sheds, one of which is the stables; another houses a mud-spattered four-wheel-drive vehicle. A large white tank contains the household's water supply and further off there are several smaller tanks, each with an attendant windmill drawing water from precious underground reserves. A kilometre or so from the homestead is a roughly circular pool that collects rainwater but will become dry during a period of extended drought. Leading from the homestead in several directions are numerous roadways – little more than corrugated tracks – that lead to the extremities of the property.

It is hard to believe, but this scene is part of agricultural Australia. It is one of many vast, isolated cattle stations in far western Queensland and the Northern Territory, some of which cover more than 1 million hectares and support herds of thousands of animals, sometimes at a density as sparse as 30 hectares per head.

Previous pages Sugar cane fields, near Gordonvale in north Queensland, are harvested.
Previous pages (inset) Crop fields near Kununurra in Western Australia need irrigation.
Opposite Windmills create a striking feature against the sky over Eungella in Queensland.

In the pioneering days, pastoral life in the arid interior was arduous, difficult and dangerous. Cattle had to be driven huge distances overland to pastures and to markets, and illness and accidents were feared as there was no easy access to medical attention. Even today, with the benefits of modern communications and greatly improved transport, the tyrannies of distance and isolation can still be keenly felt. The tedium of station life, however, is relieved by a number of regular social and cultural events which have become rituals of outback life. Among the more colourful of these occasions are the picnic race meetings and rodeos that bring people from thousands of kilometres away.

Much of the country's beef is produced under the harsh conditions of Australia's arid interior. However, in the south of the continent and in Tasmania, herds of beef cattle graze in a more benign environment and often share their grazing lands with sheep and dairy cattle. In Victoria and Tasmania, where dairy cattle constitute a high proportion of most herds, pastures are often in green and rolling countryside.

Above left *Annual race meetings in country centres attract enthusiasts from near and far. Many of the wealthier landholders fly in to the venues in their private planes, while others travel the long distances by car.*
Left and below *Birdsville in the south-western corner of Queensland has about 100 inhabitants, but the 1996 annual race meeting attracted a record crowd of more than 6000 enthusiastic competitors and supporters.*

Above Birdsville Hotel's bar enjoys brisk trade during the race weekend.
Right The annual Henley-on-Todd Regatta is run on a dry riverbed.
Below right Rodeos are fun events for both competitors and spectators.
Following pages The lush area around Berry, a quaint old agricultural town on the New South Wales south coast, is prime dairying country.

Above The remains of a 19th-century station homestead called Dalhousie still crumble in the lonely far northern region of South Australia.
Below Sheep may be transported long distances in multi-tiered trucks before being sold at country stock auctions in the Australian outback.

It used to be said that Australia rode 'on the sheep's back', an indication of the crucial importance of the wool industry to Australia's prosperity. Although wool has declined somewhat in relative importance in recent decades, it was for well over a century the mainstay of the Australian economy. Even today the country still produces a third of all the world's wool supplies.

The overwhelming majority of Australia's sheep are merinos, the heavy-fleeced breed that was introduced into New South Wales by John Macarthur in the early 1800s and which he and his wife Elizabeth bred on their property at Camden Park, south-west of Sydney. As early as the 1830s, wool had become Australia's most important export, with virtually all the wool clip being shipped to England to feed the voracious appetites of its textile mills. As the colony of New South Wales expanded westwards during the 1820s, people known as 'squatters' drove large flocks of sheep into the interior and selected tracts of land on which to establish their 'runs'. When the land on the western slopes of the range was taken up, the squatters drove their sheep further and further inland, into ever more arid country. Today, sheep farming is carried on in a wide range of landscapes and climatic zones, from moist, fertile coastal regions to dry and relatively inhospitable inland areas in western New South Wales and South Australia. There are, however, very few sheep raised in the areas of extreme wet or dry climates. Sheep are less hardy than cattle, less able to travel vast distances in search of water, and subject to footrot in very wet, humid conditions.

Australia's wool industry was born in New South Wales, and that state still has the greatest concentration of the nation's sheep. More than a third of the flocks graze on the western slopes, central-western plains and, to a lesser extent, the drier far west of the state, often sharing their pasture with beef cattle. About 35 million sheep, almost a quarter of Australia's total, are raised in Western Australia in a band that extends from near Albany in the fertile far south-west, northwards beyond Geraldton into country that can be dry, dusty and harsh. One of the pioneers of the wool industry in this area was John Hassell, who in 1849 established a sheep run on over 3000 hectares at Jerramungup in the far south. At about the same time, the explorer A.C. Gregory brought back reports of promising grazing land around Geraldton. As had happened in New South Wales, squatters drove their flocks into these and adjoining areas, laying claim to tracts of land and gradually extending the area of settlement and grazing.

Left This historic wooden woolshed at Kinchega near Menindee in far western New South Wales was once part of an enormous sheep station.
Opposite Sheep are herded into large pens at Silver Hills, north of the town of Richmond in outback north Queensland, before being shorn.

THE LARGEST OUTBACK STATION

During the late 1870s and 1880s, pastoralists moved into the present-day Northern Territory and began establishing large cattle stations there. One of the most important of these stations was that of South Australian financier-pastoralist C.B. Fisher who, with his partner J.M. Lyons, took up leases covering 88 000 square kilometres – more than twice the size of Switzerland. Included in these was a vast station on the Victoria River, 200 kilometres south-west of Katherine, known as Victoria River Downs.

From the beginning, Aboriginal stockmen were the mainstay of the outback pastoral industry. They were readily available, cheap to employ – until 1950 they were usually paid only in food, clothing and swags – and were often superb horsemen. Without them, stations could not have maintained their vast and scattered herds.

For more than 50 years, Victoria River Downs was very isolated, but this changed in 1929 when the railway line was built. Back then, it boasted its own police station, hospital and outdoor cinema, as well as many residential dwellings.

In the 1950s, stations such as Victoria River Downs were owned by overseas interests who paid no income tax on Northern Territory properties. The removal of this tax concession, combined with the granting of large tracts of the Northern Territory to traditional Aboriginal owners in the 1970s, led to the breaking up of many of the extensive cattle stations. Today, Victoria River Downs covers about one-third of its original area.

WHEAT COUNTRY

The extension of settlements from coastal areas was accompanied by the clearing of large areas of timbered country and the tilling of soils for the production of crops, by far the most important of which was wheat. In spring and early summer every year, this golden crop covers paddocks comprising about one-seventh of the Australian mainland, mainly in two wheat belts. In the east and south, the wheat belt stretches in a crescent from the western side of the Great Dividing Range in southern Queensland, through central-western New South Wales, across central and northern Victoria into southern South Australia to the edge of the arid Nullarbor Plain. In Western Australia, another belt runs in a broad sweep from south-west of Perth to the coastal region north of Geraldton. This western region produces one-third of Australia's annual wheat crop.

The wheat belts coincide generally with the major wool-producing areas and with many of the more southerly cattle-grazing regions. Of the more than 26 000 Australian farms that cultivate wheat, only about one in five grows this crop exclusively. The majority combine wheat growing with other forms of agriculture, such as barley and oats, and with grazing of stock. Wheat is very subject to the vagaries of climate and soil conditions and most farmers consider its sole cultivation as too risky an enterprise. One of the most intensively farmed areas is the so-called mallee country in western Victoria, where millions of hectares of native mallee have been cleared for the production of cereal crops, predominantly wheat. In parts of this semi-arid environment – the annual rainfall is a mere 400 millimetres – wheatlands stretch as far as the eye can see in a vast expanse of yellow gold punctuated by remnant patches of the straggly mallee.

Left Golden wheatfields seem to roll on forever at Lyndoch in South Australia's Barossa Valley, an area notable for its thriving wine industry.
Below Numerous towering wheat silos are sited at Dalby in southern Queensland, one of the richest agricultural regions on the mainland.

HARNESSING RIVERS

In 1938, Dr John Bradfield, the Brisbane engineer who was also responsible for masterminding the construction of both the Sydney Harbour Bridge and Brisbane's Story Bridge, proposed a grandiose and complex scheme to the Queensland government. His plan was to divert the waters of several north Queensland rivers inland via a series of dams and tunnels, and eventually to irrigate parts of the continent's dry centre in order to extend the pastoral regions. His visionary scheme was never implemented and was, in all probability, highly impractical. Several more modest schemes, however, have proved viable, especially in areas in southern New South Wales and north and north-western Victoria around the Murray and Murrumbidgee rivers. A series of dams has transformed large tracts in these regions from dry red earth into huge patchworks of cultivated land that are among the richest fruit- and wine-producing areas in Australia.

The Sunraysia district of far north-western Victoria, just north of the mallee country, is centred on the town of Mildura, a major dried fruit and wine area. More than half of Australia's dried fruit production comes from this region. Further to the south-east the Riverina district, covering more than a million hectares between the Murray and Lachlan rivers, has extensive orchards and vineyards and plantings of a variety of vegetables. It is also the country's major rice-growing region and the source of one-fifth of Australia's total wine production. This thriving agricultural region is a far cry from the country which the explorer John Oxley saw in 1817 and which he described as 'desolate plains' that would probably not 'ever again be visited by civilised man'. In spite of this grim prediction, Oxley, perhaps with some uncanny premonition of the area's distant agricultural future, planted seeds of various stone fruits before he left the region.

Above Watermelons grow in rich soil near Kununurra in north-western Western Australia, and are irrigated by the Ord River Irrigation Scheme. *Below* Masses of grapes drying in the sun near Mildura in north-western Victoria are sold as raisins, an important Australian export industry.

Above The main crop grown around Mareeba in north Queensland is tobacco, but sweet potatoes, coffee and mangoes are also widely cultivated. *Below* Grapes are grown extensively throughout the Murrumbidgee Irrigation Area to support Griffith's thriving wine-making industry.

QUEENSLAND'S DARLING DOWNS

Ten years after Oxley's expedition to the future Riverina, Allan Cunningham led an expedition to the north from Segenhoe, northwest of Newcastle in New South Wales. After two months, he came upon what he described as a tract of 'superior country', covered with an 'extraordinary luxuriance of growth'. Cunningham named this land the Darling Downs, after the governor of New South Wales.

The rich black soil of these plains and valleys, which lie about 160 kilometres west of Brisbane and extend for approximately 12 000 square kilometres with the Great Dividing Range forming their northeast boundary, now supports a great diversity of crops, from fruit and vegetables to cotton. But its chief claim to fame is as the producer of perhaps Australia's finest quality wheat. Viewed from the air, the Darling Downs present the classic agricultural vista, a great network of contrasting patterns in a range of diverse shades.

A COASTAL FEAST

In Victoria and southern New South Wales stone, berry and citrus fruits grow, supplying the region with a valuable source of income. Australia is one of the largest producers of dried fruit in the world, while Tasmania is often nicknamed the 'Apple Isle'. Sugar cane was first grown near Brisbane in 1862 and is now a major crop in the coastal stretch from Mossman in the north to the Clarence River in New South Wales. Early in the late 19th century, Kanakas were forcibly indentured from the South Sea Islands to work on the fields and much of the success of the industry is due to them and the Italian immigrants who followed in their wake. Today, Australia is the world's third-largest exporter of raw sugar. A variety of tropical fruits also grows along the Queensland–New South Wales fertile coastal strip. Queensland is often referred to as the 'Banana State', yet the majority of that crop's yield comes from New South Wales.

Above Bananas grow prolifically in the fertile soil around semi-tropical Coffs Harbour on the east coast, halfway between Sydney and Brisbane.
Below Bundaberg in south-eastern Queensland produces both sugar and rum. About one-fifth of Australia's sugar is produced in this famous region.

Above The Big Pineapple is a landmark at Nambour in south-eastern Queensland where it boldly proclaims one of the area's main crops.
Below Sugar cane ablaze in south-eastern Queensland. The cane is often burnt before harvesting commences to drive out vermin and snakes.

AND SOMETHING TO DRINK

Captain Arthur Phillip, the first governor of the British colony of New South Wales, planted grapes on Australian soil at Farm Cove in 1788. Three years later, Phillip organised a more substantial planting west of Sydney at Parramatta. Since then, wine production has developed into one of Australia's most important primary industries and, particularly since the late 1980s, has become a major source of export income.

The modern wine industry in Australia can be traced back to the early 1830s when a Scotsman, James Busby, planted vine cuttings collected in France and Spain on his Kirkton Estate in the Hunter Valley, north of Sydney. This area now boasts more than 50 wineries.

Some of the first plantings in South Australia's Barossa Valley, north-east of Adelaide, were taken from Busby's original cuttings. German immigrants in the 1840s and 1850s provided the main impetus for the region's wine industry. Today, the German influence in the Barossa Valley is still very much in evidence. Covering 240 square kilometres, it produces a quarter of Australia's annual wine production. Today, wine grapes are cultivated in many of the country's temperate regions, and superb wines come from as far afield as the Margaret River in Western Australia, Rutherglen in north-western Victoria, southern Queensland and even eastern Tasmania.

Above Oak barrels and an old wine press are part of a tourist display in the sales room of a winery in the Hunter Valley in New South Wales.
Below German settlers planted the first vines at Tanunda in 1847; today, the beautiful Barossa Valley is Australia's top wine-producing region.
Opposite Sweeping views of grapevines, near the town of Tanunda in South Australia, illustrate how the crop is grown in neat, regulated rows.

RIVERS,

LAKES AND

WETLANDS

RIVERS, LAKES
AND WETLANDS

*I*f statistical evidence were needed to verify the dryness of the Australian continent, the following is surely convincing: the world's largest river, the Amazon in South America, discharges 254 times the amount of water deposited into the Southern Ocean by the Murray River. Yet the Murray is Australia's greatest river, draining a vast area of the continent from southern Queensland to south-eastern South Australia. In the far north of the continent during the wet season rivers swell and vast amounts of water inundate the surrounding countryside, yet the total amount of water discharged into the sea by these northern rivers is still only 10 times the amount discharged by the Murray River.

THE BIG WET

Between December and April monsoonal downpours descend on Australia's tropical north. The landscapes right across the continent's Top End undergo a dramatic metamorphosis as the rivers in Cape York and around the Gulf of Carpentaria create vast expanses of flooded wetlands. During the dry months these streams are merely muddy channels that meander lazily across mangrove-covered plains of mud and salt flats. During the wet season this surreal environment is largely inaccessible by land and is best appreciated from the air.

In the far north-east, land on both sides of the Great Dividing Range slopes gently towards the Pacific Ocean and the Gulf of Carpentaria. During the downpour, rather than becoming raging torrents, the rivers in this region expand outwards to fill the plains with water, which in many places become impossible to traverse. As the rivers approach the coast, the silt-laden waters often converge to produce huge tidal swamps that merge with the sea of the Gulf. In some places the great quantities of silt which are deposited slowly push the coast further out into the Gulf of Carpentaria. On the east coast of the Cape York Peninsula, for example, the Normanby and Laura rivers combine to flow into Princess Charlotte Bay. The silt carried by these two rivers is slowly filling the bay, expanding the marshy, mangrove-lined fringes of the original shoreline.

Previous pages *Shrouded in morning mist, Tasmania's Gordon River is a peaceful sight.*
Previous pages (inset) *Pelicans have made a home at Lake Bonney in South Australia.*
Opposite *The Tully River in north Queensland is an exciting spot for white-water rafting.*

The 537000-hectare Lakefield National Park, located on the Cape York Peninsula, is bounded to the east by the Normanby River and the shores of Princess Charlotte Bay and is traversed by several rivers. During the dry season, it becomes a wilderness of swamps and lagoons that offers wonderful insights into the nature of this unique area as well as opportunities for bushwalking and canoeing. Care, however, is needed as these waters are home to the dangerous saltwater crocodile as well as the smaller and more innocuous freshwater species.

Top Only four-wheel-drives can negotiate the Old Telegraph Track in the Jardine River National Park near the tip of the Cape York Peninsula.
Above Waterlilies grow in abundance on the tranquil Horseshoe Lagoon in the Lakefield National Park, renowned for its prehistoric rock art.
Right When in flood, the Millstream Falls near Ravenshoe in the north of Queensland are said to be among the wildest rapids in Australia.
Opposite Noted for its succession of treacherous rapids, the turbulent Tully River flows into the Pacific south of Innisfail in north Queensland.

THE WONDERS OF ARNHEM LAND

East of Darwin is the wild and ancient Arnhem Land. Most of Arnhem Land's almost 100 000 square kilometres consist of a vast raised sandstone plateau which, at its highest point, is 500 metres above sea level. At its western extremity this great plateau ends abruptly in a 600-kilometre-long rocky escarpment that runs north–south and rises 300 metres above an expanse of wooded plains. A number of streams, most notably the East and South Alligator rivers and their tributaries, commence on this plateau. Swollen by the wet-season monsoons, these rivers plunge dramatically over the escarpment in a series of thundering waterfalls and flood the plains. These torrents, along with other elemental forces, erode the face of the escarpment, causing it to retract south-eastwards at the rate of about 1 metre every 1000 years. Standing as evidence of this slow retreat are a number of outliers of uneroded rock that dot the plains, marking places where the escarpment once existed. Most spectacular of these is Mount Brockman, a towering mass of multi-hued sandstone that is a place of great spiritual significance to Aboriginal people.

When the rains subside the waters drain away and the plains become parched and dry. During the dry season the waters retract to a series of swamps and waterholes, many of them covered with colourful waterlilies and fringed with stands of paperbark trees. The formerly swift-flowing rivers become sluggish and then completely still. It is then, perhaps paradoxically, that the area bursts into vibrant life as the spectacular bird life converges on the remaining water, competing for the fish and other marine species that are trapped in the pools.

Below An array of Aboriginal rock art adorns the cliffs in Arnhem Land. Painted figures, such as the red ochre 'Mimi' figure (right) and the Lightning Brothers (left), represent the spirits of the great ancestors.
Opposite Waterfalls, fed by monsoonal rains during the wet season, plunge over the Arnhem Land escarpment into deep, dark waterholes.
Following pages The Top End's rocky outcrops are rich in rock paintings, but are inaccessible during the wet season when the plains are flooded.

TIDDALICK THE FROG

Stories of Tiddalick the Frog are widely told throughout Aboriginal communities, though they vary from tribe to tribe. One version from eastern Australia explains the origins of rivers and lakes, and of the frog's characteristic croak.

Long ago, all the world's water was swallowed by a gigantic frog known as Tiddalick. Fearful that everyone would die of thirst and that nothing would be able to grow, it was decided that if Tiddalick could be made to laugh he would be forced to bring up all the water. A worm crept up on Tiddalick and tickled him. The giant frog opened his mouth, bellowed with laughter, and torrents of water issued forth with such force that rivers flowed, waterfalls gushed and lakes and waterholes filled up. Everyone drank their fill and the formerly parched land began to bloom. Tiddalick, however, could not stop laughing. He laughed so loud and for so long that he lost his voice, and the only sound that he could make was the harsh croak that all frogs still make to this day.

In a similar version of the story, told by Kurnai people from the Gippsland region of Victoria, Tiddalick's amusement is caused by a dancing eel and the issuing waters create a devastating flood in which many are drowned. Others are rescued by a black pelican. However, when the pelican is rejected by a female he desires, he daubs himself with white clay and is turned into stone, becoming what is now a small island, White Rock, off the southern Victorian coast. Since that time pelicans have all been black and white.

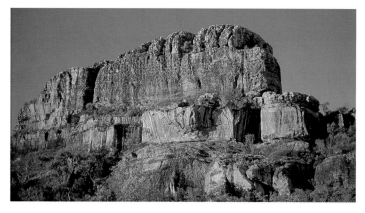

KAKADU

It is during the dry season, from May through to September, that large numbers of tourists come to the area, mainly to the Kakadu National Park. Australia's largest national park covers almost 20 000 square kilometres and includes all the region's most notable natural features. It is at Kakadu that one of the world's greatest concentrations of bird life can be observed; the range of waterbirds, especially, is bewildering and includes numerous species of ducks, herons, swamphens, egrets, ibises and stilts. There are also long-legged brolgas, noted for their flamboyant courtship dances, and jabirus, Australia's only storks, unmistakable with their long red legs, huge black pointed bills and fluorescent blue-green necks and heads.

In addition to the waterbirds, there is a great variety of birds of prey, from regal wedge-tailed eagles to small sparrowhawks, as well as many parrots and honeyeaters attracted to the nectar-laden blossoms of the paperbark trees. Also conspicuous in Kakadu are no fewer than 26 species of bat, and large groups of antilopine wallaroos, marsupials that closely resemble the more common red kangaroo but which live only in the extreme north of the continent. Rather incongruous in this sanctuary of native animals is the water buffalo, which was imported from Asia last century as a draught animal and source of meat, and thrived and proliferated in the region.

Above *Ubirr's rocky outcrops contain a treasury of Aboriginal rock art and provide high points from which to survey the surrounding landscape.*
Opposite top *Nourlangie Rock in Kakadu National Park is an excellent example of how the sandstone escarpment has been eroded by flood waters.*
Opposite bottom *A scenic boat trip on the languid waters of the Yellow Waters Lagoon is a great way to explore Kakadu National Park.*

Below left *The lotus bird is about the size of a small fowl and is one of many species of waterbirds found in Kakadu. It is also commonly referred to as the Christbird, or lily-trotter, because its long radiating toes enable it to walk easily across large, sturdy leaves on the surface of the water.*
Below *Water buffalo, which were introduced from Timor in 1820, now roam wild in many parts of Kakadu National Park.*

RIVER BOATS ON THE MURRAY RIVER

During the second half of the 19th century, the waters of the Murray, Darling and Murrumbidgee rivers were plied by a variety of craft transporting people, goods and agricultural produce to and from Australia's inland areas. Roads were either rough and ready or, in some places, non-existent and the bullock wagons that were the main form of inland transport were slow and uncomfortable. In the great age of steam, and in the absence of a far-reaching railway system, the rivers were the highways of the interior. From the 1850s, 20 years after Charles Sturt's pioneering journeys of river exploration, more paddle-steamers made their way up and down the rivers, not only conveying people and goods, but promoting trade and opening up previously inaccessible areas for development. Large barges, drawn by paddle-steamers, were laden with wool bales sent from inland stations and bound for points along the rivers from where they could be taken to Sydney and other major cities. Barges also frequently carried piles of timber. Towards the end of the century, the expanding railways began to supplant the role of the steamers. Echuca, on the Murray, was the centre of the river trade and as late as the turn of the century was Australia's largest inland port. Its famous wharf, built of red gum, was a kilometre long, and had three levels to allow for fluctuations in the level of the river. In more recent times, the old paddle-steamers have been refurbished and put back into service to cater for a burgeoning tourist trade.

THE MURRAY–DARLING RIVER SYSTEM

The Murray–Darling system is one of the world's great river systems, but it has a much smaller discharge than any other comparable one. A high rate of evaporation, the very gentle gradient of the land through which it travels and the quantities of water that are taken from the river to irrigate farmland also contribute to the paucity of its flow. Indeed, if its riverbed were of sand rather than of hard clay, the Murray would no doubt suffer the fate of many other inland streams and simply dry up well short of its destination.

The Murray is Australia's longest, grandest river and forms much of the boundary between New South Wales and Victoria. It begins its 2500-kilometre journey as little more than a creek in the Snowy Mountains. As it tumbles down the slopes it gathers strength from mountain streams and creeks, often swelled by melting snow, until it reaches the flat country where it loops its way through irrigated farmlands, then past wooded banks, and finally through a limestone gorge, after which it empties unspectacularly into Lake Alexandrina, just east of St Vincents Gulf in south-east South Australia. On its way, the Murray is joined by the Murrumbidgee which, with its major tributary, the Lachlan, drains large sections of western New South Wales and, more significantly, the Darling River.

The Darling is the great river of western New South Wales. It begins its 2700-kilometre southward journey in southern Queensland where it is known successively by various names until, just north of Bourke,

in north-western New South Wales, it becomes decisively the Darling. As it flows sluggishly southwards, the Darling is joined by several tributaries from the semi-arid west of New South Wales, including the Bogan, Castlereagh and Namoi rivers – streams that flow west from the Great Dividing Range. At one point the Darling itself spreads lazily into a number of streams – called 'anabranches' – some of which trail off into swamps and lakes. The Darling joins the Murray at Wentworth near the Victoria–New South Wales border.

For the greater part of its length, the banks of the Murray are bordered by thick growths of stately river red gums, which in places extend to forests 25 kilometres wide. Regular floods help ensure the survival of these handsome eucalypts. As the river nears its end, however, scrubby multi-stemmed mallee predominates. By the time the Murray enters Lake Alexandrina, still almost 80 kilometres from the sea, its banks are bordered mainly by bare saltbush plains which merge into tidal salt flats. The great inland explorer Charles Sturt, who in 1829–30 led the first expedition to follow the Murray River to the sea, described the huge freshwater lake into which the river rather limply flows after traversing a long stretch of 'barren and sandy' wasteland as: 'a beautiful lake ... a fitting reservoir for the noble stream that has led us to it'.

While the Murray is indeed a noble stream, it is certainly not a limpid one; for much of its length it is muddy brown. Despite this, its waters teem with many species of native fish, most notably the famous Murray cod, a giant that can grow to more than a metre and a half long. It was this fish that sustained Sturt's expedition as it made its tortuous progress along the river. Birds, mammals and a variety of reptiles also thrive in the forests that are nourished by the river as it flows through an otherwise arid environment.

Above The slow-flowing Darling River meanders through the Kinchega National Park, south of the Menindee Lakes in western New South Wales. *Opposite* In recent years a number of houseboats have appeared on the Murray River, providing a popular form of accommodation for tourists.

153

A HAVEN FOR PELICANS

An Aboriginal story tells of a man who pursued a cod along the length of the Murray River. As he chased the fish, the song he sang created the river. When he eventually approached the sea, he caught the giant fish, which splashed so violently in its attempts to escape that it created a great lake. That lake is Lake Alexandrina, and its waters spilled over to form the adjacent Lake Albert as well as a whole series of lagoons stretching for 130 kilometres to the south-east. It also forms one of Australia's richest wetland environments, the Coorong.

The lagoons of the Coorong are up to 2 kilometres wide and are set among sand dunes. They become progressively narrower, shallower and saltier until at their south-eastern extremity they tail off into saline marshes that are much saltier than the sea. The sea is never far away, for this sheltered wilderness is protected from the thundering surf of the Southern Ocean only by the shifting sand dunes of the Younghusband Peninsula. It is an eerily beautiful landscape and an environment that sustained and nourished local Aboriginal people for many thousands of years.

The lagoons are filled with many species of fish, while wombats and emus roam the surrounding heathlands. But it is as a bird sanctuary that the Coorong is most noted. More than 160 species of waterbirds breed on the islands between the lagoons, including the largest colony of pelicans anywhere in Australia. Brolgas, albatrosses, cormorants, gulls and grebes – these and countless others are among the residents and visitors to the region. In times of drought there is an explosion of bird life as flocks fly in from hitherto watered inland areas.

TASMANIA'S WILD WEST

After the monsoonal far north, the south-west of Tasmania is the wettest region in Australia. The harsh and mountainous terrain has helped to guarantee its preservation as a largely unspoilt wilderness. Unlike the gentler countryside on the eastern side of the island, much of the west coast is inhospitable to human exploration. Indeed, it is only in the last half-century that parts of this forbidding landscape of wild rivers, rocky mountain ranges and treacherous shorelines have been charted and recorded. The entrance to the only safe haven along its coast, the extensive Macquarie Harbour, is through a narrow and hazardous headland known as Hells Gates.

The rivers that rise in the high, rocky reaches of the Central Plateau plunge down the slopes and flow swiftly, at times over treacherous rapids, through steep, narrow chasms and, in their lower reaches, past stands of dense rainforests. The most substantial of these rivers are the Gordon and the Franklin, which converge for the last 30 kilometres of their journey and flow together as the Gordon River into the south-east extremity of Macquarie Harbour.

These two rivers became the centre of bitter controversy and the focus of international attention in the early 1980s when government and environmentalists clashed over plans to exploit their waters for the generation of electricity. More than 10 years earlier, the Gordon had been dammed in its upper reaches as the first part of a projected Gordon River hydro-electric scheme. As a result of this controversial development, one of the highland lakes in western Tasmania, Lake Pedder, had been flooded. Perched picturesquely among mountain peaks and rocky outcrops, and considered by many to be the most beautiful of them all, Lake Pedder's most distinguishing feature had been a superb beach of white sand that fringed its shores.

In 1980 plans were announced to build another dam, this time across the Gordon below its junction with the Franklin River. There was a huge organised campaign against the scheme, which would have flooded the two river valleys for a distance of more than 100 kilometres, obliterating forever some of the finest scenery in the country as well as some sites of great archaeological significance. Arguments raged, blockades were put in place and 1272 protesters were arrested before the Australian federal government enacted legislation to prevent the building of the dam.

Above Pelicans are common on most Australian waterways, but they are nowhere as abundant as in the Coorong on the South Australian coast.
Opposite Subdued light and deep water reflections turn the isolated Butler Island in Tasmania's Gordon River into a scene of mystery.
Following pages Macquarie Harbour, on the south-west coast of Tasmania, extends 32 kilometres inland to the mouth of the Gordon River. Its mountainous shoreline is lined with lush, dense forests.

PICTURE CREDITS

All photographs by **Shaen Adey** *(NHIL) apart from those listed below: *Biblioteca Apostolica Vaticana* p. 18 (top) **Jane Burton Taylor** pp. 146 (left and right), 147, 148–149 *Coo-ee Historical Photographic Library* p. 20 (top) **Denise Greig** (NHIL) p. 25 (top centre) **Ian Hutton** pp. 98 (top and bottom), 99 **Anthony Johnson** (NHIL) front cover, pp. 1, 10, 19 (top left), 20 (bottom left), 29, 34 (top right), 36, 37 (top), 40 (top and bottom), 44, 46 (top and bottom, left and right), 50 (top), 53 (top), 59 (bottom left), 76, 81 (top), 82 (top left), 84, 114 (bottom, left and right), 151 (bottom, left and right) **NHIL** pp. 24 (bottom), 25 (top right), 43 (bottom right), 107 (top right), 113, 136 (bottom right) **Photo Access Photographic Library (Doug Perrine)** p. 88 (top and bottom) **Nick Rains** (NHIL) pp. 34 (top left and bottom right), 105 (right), 112, 138 (top) **Rebecca Saunders** pp. 80, 81 (bottom) **Joe Shemesh** pp. 73, 114 (top), 120, 121 (bottom), 140, 155, 156–157 **Western Australia Department of Land Administration** (image courtesy of Robert Shaw) p. 12 **Wetro-Pics Photographic Library (Mike Prociv)** p. 119 (top).

* NHIL = New Holland Image Library